DAVID HAIG

David Haig has written two stage plays for Hampstead Theatre, London: *My Boy Jack* and *The Good Samaritan*, both critically acclaimed. *My Boy Jack* was filmed for ITV, starring David, Daniel Radcliffe and Kim Cattrall, and broadcast in November 2007.

His distinguished acting career includes West End appearances in *Art*, *Dead Funny* (a transfer from Hampstead), *Journey's End*, *The Country Wife* and *The Sea*. At the National Theatre he appeared in Alan Ayckbourn's *House/Garden*, and at the Royal Court in *Hitchcock Blonde* and *The Recruiting Officer*. He has worked extensively for the Royal Shakespeare Company, playing, amongst others, Angelo in Trevor Nunn's production of *Measure for Measure*. He won the Olivier Award for Best Actor for *Our Country's Good* at the Royal Court, and received nominations for *Mary Poppins* and *Donkeys' Years*, both in the West End.

His television and film appearances include *Four Weddings and a Funeral*, *The Thin Blue Line*, *Talking Heads* and *Crime and Punishment*.

Other Titles by Nick Hern Books

David Haig

MY BOY JACK

NICK HERN BOOKS
London
www.nickhernbooks.co.uk

A Nick Hern Book

My Boy Jack first published in Great Britain as a paperback original in 1997 by Nick Hern Books Limited, The Glasshouse, 49a Goldhawk Road, London W12 8QP

Reprinted in this edition 2007, 2008, 2010, 2011, 2012

My Boy Jack copyright © 1997 David Haig

David Haig has asserted his right to be identified as the author of this work

Typeset by Country Setting, Kingsdown, Kent CT14 8ES
Printed in Great Britain by Mimeo Ltd, Cambridgeshire PE29 6XX

A CIP catalogue record for this book is available from the British Library

ISBN 978 1 85459 583 6

My Boy Jack opened at Hampstead Theatre, London, on 13 October 1997. First preview was 9 October. The cast was as follows:

RUDYARD KIPLING	David Haig
CARRIE KIPLING	Belinda Lang
JOHN ('Jack') KIPLING	John Light
ELSIE ('Bird') KIPLING	Sarah Howe
GUARDSMAN BOWE	Billy Carter
GUARDSMAN DOYLE, COL. RORY POTTLE, MR. FRANKLAND	Fred Ridgeway
GUARDSMAN McHUGH, MAJOR SPARKS	Dermot Kerrigan

Director   John Dove
Designer   Michael Taylor
Artistic Director   Jenny Topper

MY BOY JACK

Characters

RUDYARD KIPLING	Mid-forties, wiry, energetic, walrus moustache, huge eyebrows, balding, spectacles
CARRIE KIPLING	Rudyard's wife. Mid-forties, short, handsome, somewhat formidable
JOHN ('JACK') KIPLING	Rudyard's son. Sixteen years old at the beginning of the play. Tall, gangly, and extremely short-sighted
ELSIE ('BIRD') KIPLING	John's older sister. Eighteen years old at the beginning of the play. Intelligent, forthright, inquisitive
GUARDSMAN BOWE GUARDSMAN McHUGH GUARDSMAN DOYLE	Members of John's platoon of Irish Guards
MR. FRANKLAND	A friend of Guardsman Bowe
MAJOR SPARKS	An Army Doctor
COL. RORY POTTLE	Representative of the Army Medical Board

The play requires a cast of seven actors

ACT ONE SCENE ONE

September 1913.

Drawing room. 'Batemans.' RUDYARD KIPLING's home in Sussex. In the room is a book case, a long table, and an oak cabinet, above which hangs a large oil portrait of a six-year-old girl.

RUDYARD is alone. He is opening a parcel. In it are the scores of several Music Hall songs.

RUDYARD. Oh, good.

He places the music on the table, and gleefully lights a cigarette. He picks up one of the scores.

Oh good, good, good, good, good, good, good, good.

As he reads the score, he taps out a rhythm and hums tunelessly. He stops for a moment, looks at his watch, goes to the door and shouts upstairs.

Come on Jack, let's be having you, we're up against it!

He returns to his music and starts to sing – badly. Half way through the rendition, RUDYARD's son JOHN enters. Unnoticed, he listens to his father sing.

'When I take my morning promenade,
Quite a fashion card, on the Promenade.
Oh! I don't mind nice boys staring hard,
If it satisfies their desire.

'Do you think my dress is a little bit,
Just a little bit – well not too much of it,
Tho' it shows my shape just a little bit,
That's the little bit the boys admire.'

JOHN. Daddo . . . ?

RUDYARD. At last! Let's have a look at you.

JOHN. Excellent song.

RUDYARD. 'Tis a good one.

JOHN. Which is it?

RUDYARD. You know it don't you?

JOHN. Do I?

RUDYARD. *When I Take My Morning Promenade*.

JOHN. Oh, yes.

RUDYARD. Didn't you recognise it?

JOHN. Well . . .

RUDYARD. That does not say much for the voice.

JOHN. Perhaps I'd have got it if it was the chorus.

RUDYARD. I absolutely was singing the chorus.

JOHN. Oh. Sorry.

RUDYARD. Anyway.

JOHN. It is usually sung by a woman, so . . .

RUDYARD. Jack – close subject. Let's have a proper look at you. Aren't you excited old man?

JOHN. I don't know what to expect.

RUDYARD. Well, they'll check you over, they might want a bit of a chat . . . (*He looks at* JOHN*'s suit.*) The kit is first-rate . . . where's your pince-nez?

JOHN. I can't get to grips with it.

RUDYARD. Well you must. They give a man a different expression as compared to spectacles.

JOHN. It won't stay on my nose.

RUDYARD. Have you got it about you?

JOHN. I think so.

RUDYARD. Well, let's have a look – Pop it on.

JOHN. I don't want to wear it.

RUDYARD. Jack, we need the overall impression. Pop it on please.

JOHN *blearily removes his spectacles. He puts the pince-nez on.*

JOHN. It doesn't suit me.

RUDYARD. Yes it does. Turn to the side. Face me. I think it's good. I wonder if you shouldn't brush your hair back, away from the face?

JOHN. Why?

RUDYARD. You've got a high forehead, it'd be a shame to waste it.

JOHN. What's a high forehead got to do with it?

RUDYARD. It's a sign of intelligence.

JOHN. It can't be.

RUDYARD. I am assured it is . . . here's a comb – give it a try.

JOHN *does so*.

Where's mi baccy? (*He locates his pipe*.) Let me tell you the programme, you go before the Army Medical Board at three o'clock this afternoon.

JOHN. Who'll be there?

RUDYARD. An army doctor, probably someone on the board . . . it's just a preliminary canter, I'm sure it'll be thoroughly undaunting. And afterwards we celebrate – we head for the Alhambra.

JOHN *has brushed his hair and balanced the pince-nez on his nose, to ensure that it stays in place he has to stand with his head back and his chin in the air.*

JOHN. There.

RUDYARD. I like that!

JOHN. What will they want to chat about?

RUDYARD. Well, . . . I tell you what, let's have a little rehearsal. I'll fire a couple of basic questions at you, and you answer me as naturally as you can . . . wearing the pince-nez . . .

JOHN. No.

RUDYARD. Why not?

JOHN. Do I have to?

RUDYARD. Of course we don't have to . . . it's not for my benefit.

JOHN. Oh don't be like that Daddo. Let's do it then, ask me a question.

RUDYARD. Not if you don't think it's going to help.

JOHN. I do, I do. Please ask me.

RUDYARD. I think it'll be useful.

JOHN. It will.

RUDYARD. I'm not doing this for fun. It's for your sake.

JOHN. I know.

RUDYARD. Alright. First question. John, why are you so keen to join the Army?

JOHN. Well . . . the army needs volunteers . . . I can't balance the thing . . .

RUDYARD. All the more reason to practice now. Concentrate. Yes, the Army needs volunteers – why?

JOHN. Um . . . it needs volunteers because Germany has been preparing for war . . . for years . . . and . . .

RUDYARD. Specify. How many years?

JOHN. Um . . . (*Silence.*)

RUDYARD. Well, her intentions were clear as long ago as 1870. 1870 to 1913 is?

JOHN. Um, forty years.

RUDYARD. Nearer forty-five isn't it?

JOHN. Do I need to say that?

RUDYARD. Absolutely, yes. Facts at your fingertips. Go on.

JOHN. It won't stay on Daddo.

RUDYARD. It's good Jack, keep going.

JOHN. I feel ridiculous.

RUDYARD. Keep going.

JOHN. I've always wanted to join the Navy or the Army.

RUDYARD. Don't mention the Navy old man!

JOHN. No.

RUDYARD. Recipe for disaster! Carry on.

JOHN. I've always wanted to join the Army, and to, . . . what's the word? . . . er . . . save, or . . . hold on to our . . .

RUDYARD. Preserve?

JOHN. Hold on to our preserve?

RUDYARD. No, no! – 'Hold on to,' 'preserve'.

JOHN. Oh, I see . . . preserve our . . . (*The pince-nez topples off his nose.*) You see! Much too loose. My nose simply doesn't suit the thing.

He scrumples up his hair and strides off, throwing the pince-nez on the floor.

RUDYARD. Careful! (*He rescues the pince-nez.*)

JOHN. I can't see how this will make any difference to my chances. If the Army is desperate for recruits they won't mind a pair of specs.

RUDYARD. Jack, the Navy has already rejected you once. Your eyes are a serious stumbling block. Your performance this afternoon is very important, and the first impression you give is vital. You've got to take a big pull on yourself and really dig out.

JOHN. I'm doing my best Daddo. I won't let you down.

RUDYARD. I know . . . perhaps if I . . . bend this in a little . . . (*He holds up the pince-nez and adjusts it.*) Jack, here a moment . . . (JACK *walks over to his father.*) Let's see if we can't . . .

He is about to place the pince-nez on his son's nose. But suddenly he stops. He has noticed something on JACK*'s forehead.*

A chicken pox scar.

JOHN. I've always had that.

RUDYARD. I've never noticed it before. (RUDYARD *touches it gently with his finger.*) It's the shape of a tiny horse shoe. It's the right way up, it'll bring you luck.

JOHN. Will it?

RUDYARD. Absolutely . . . see if that's a snugger fit.

RUDYARD *places the pince-nez on his son's nose.*

Better?

JOHN. Probably.

RUDYARD. What makes you think you'd make a good soldier?

JOHN. Daddo –

RUDYARD. What makes you think you'd make a good soldier?

JOHN. I've always wanted to join the Army, to fight for my country, and to er . . . preserve our . . .

Again the pince-nez falls off. JOHN *lets out a scream of frustration.*

I – CAN'T – DO IT!

RUDYARD. You can Jack.

JOHN. I've done my best.

RUDYARD. Not quite.

JOHN. I'm not wearing it.

RUDYARD. Come on.

JOHN. I – am – not – wearing it.

RUDYARD. Once more.

JOHN. No.

RUDYARD. Once more.

JOHN. No.

RUDYARD*'s wife* CARRIE *has heard the scream and appears at the door carrying a bunch of freshly picked flowers.*

CARRIE. Rud . . .

RUDYARD. No. Not now. Please.

CARRIE. What have you been doing?

RUDYARD. Out! Now! We're absolutely fine. Please.

CARRIE. I just want to change Josie's flowers.

RUDYARD. Could you do it later please, it's not a good moment.

CARRIE. What's the matter?

JOHN. Nothing.

RUDYARD. We're fine.

CARRIE (*to* JOHN). Why are you upset?

JOHN. I'm not.

CARRIE *swaps the fresh flowers for the old ones under Josie's portrait.*

RUDYARD. Can you do them later please, we're plum in the middle of something.

CARRIE *goes to* JOHN. *She is holding the old flowers which drip dirty water.*

CARRIE (*touching* JOHN*'s face*). Look at me. You mustn't volunteer for our sake.

JOHN. You're dripping onto your skirt.

CARRIE. Are you listening?

JOHN. Mother, you're dripping water onto your new skirt.

RUDYARD. I'm getting very angry.

CARRIE (*to* JOHN). You've plenty of time to decide.

JOHN. I've already decided.

CARRIE. There's no hurry.

JOHN. Daddo thinks there is.

CARRIE (*to* RUDYARD). He's fifteen.

RUDYARD. Nearly sixteen.

CARRIE. He's too young.

RUDYARD. He is not a boy, he is a young man. If you continue to pamper and paw him, you will turn him into something altogether weak and watery . . . the next few hours will be a serious point in his career.

CARRIE. Do you think it's fair to encourage him?

RUDYARD. I would think it very unfair if I didn't. Within a year, by the end of 1914, we shall be fighting for civilisation itself, one wouldn't want him to miss an opportunity to be part of that.

CARRIE. His eyes are not just an excuse . . . We should wait.

RUDYARD. No we shouldn't.

CARRIE. But why? You seem to be the only person in the country who believes Germany will fight.

RUDYARD. Rubbish.

CARRIE. You can't drag a fifteen-year-old boy . . .

JOHN. I am in the room, I'm not a cripple.

CARRIE. Of course you're not, but please let's remember, the Navy gave you five minutes! Five minutes and you were booted out, and on your way home.

RUDYARD. When will people wake up? We don't have much time. I want Jack –

CARRIE. *You* want.

RUDYARD. For his sake.

CARRIE. No it's for your sake.

RUDYARD. It's nothing to do with me, it's Jack's future.

CARRIE. No.

RUDYARD. I'm not going to argue. (*Gesturing at the door.*)
    Carrie, please.

CARRIE. Jack –

RUDYARD. No.

CARRIE. Just –

RUDYARD. No.

> CARRIE *goes to the door. She stops. After a moment.*

CARRIE. I've done the mail. I'd like you to sign two cheques.

RUDYARD. Fine.

CARRIE. There was a begging letter from the 'Army Welfare
    Fund'. I've sent them £15 on your behalf.

RUDYARD. Thank you.

CARRIE. Be gentle. (*She leaves.*)

RUDYARD (*supportively*). I'm on your side old man, you know
    that don't you?

> JOHN *nods but says nothing.*

> Come here . . . (RUDYARD *puts an arm round* JOHN's
> *shoulder.*) . . . it will pay dividends . . . buck up now.

JOHN. I'll have another go.

RUDYARD. Good idea . . . well done.

JOHN. I've always wanted to join the Army, and to fight for my
    country. I think it's particularly important at the moment that as
    many young men as possible come forward to volunteer. The
    Germans have been preparing for war for the last forty-five
    years, and unless we act quickly, we won't be ready for them.

RUDYARD. Good. Good. Well done old man!

> *He pumps* JOHN's *hand, thrilled by his progress.*

> *End of Scene One.*

ACT ONE SCENE TWO

Later the same day.

A room at the headquarters of the Army Medical Board in London. Major SPARKS, *an army doctor, is setting up an ancient record player. Colonel* POTTLE *of the A.M.B. appears at the door, carrying a file.*

POTTLE. He's here.

SPARKS. Is he?

POTTLE. On his way over.

SPARKS. Right . . . (SPARKS *picks up a gramophone record and places it on the turntable.*) I've got rather a fun surprise for him . . . have you seen one of these? (*He indicates the record player.*)

POTTLE. It's a phonograph.

SPARKS. Spot on.

SPARKS *starts to unpack his medical bag, which contains a stethoscope etc.*

Ever met him?

POTTLE. Never.

SPARKS. Gives one the collywobbles.

POTTLE. It does.

SPARKS (*searching in his bag*). Where's the . . . ah! (*Out comes a reflex hammer.*)

There is a knock at the door. RUDYARD *pops his head round.*

RUDYARD. May we . . . ?

SPARKS. Of course, of course, come in.

RUDYARD *and* JOHN *enter.* JOHN*'s pince-nez is precariously balanced on his nose.* SPARKS *shakes* RUDYARD*'s hand.*

Charles Sparks. I shall be giving your son the once-over, and this is Colonel Rory Pottle, representing the Army Medical Board.

RUDYARD. How do you do.

POTTLE. This is a tremendous honour sir.

RUDYARD. Thank you . . . my son.

> RUDYARD *introduces* JOHN. *As rehearsed in the morning, he shakes hands vigorously with both men.*

JOHN (*to* POTTLE). How do you do sir.

POTTLE. How do you do. So you're our soldier eh?

JOHN. Yes sir. (*To* SPARKS.) How do you do sir.

SPARKS. Good to have you on board young man.

> *An awkward little silence.*

POTTLE. Good journey?

RUDYARD. Three hours, door to door.

POTTLE. From?

RUDYARD. Burwash, Sussex.

POTTLE. Ah.

SPARKS. Straight through to Charing Cross?

RUDYARD. We drove.

SPARKS. You're a motorist?

RUDYARD. Oh, yes.

POTTLE. Are you? So am I. What do you drive?

RUDYARD. Rolls Royce.

POTTLE. Really? Model?

RUDYARD. Let's, just, hold our fire. It is John's day.

SPARKS. Ah, yes.

RUDYARD. How do you want to do this Sparks?

SPARKS. Well . . . John why don't you get your togs off, and we'll have a look at the physical gubbins.

JOHN. Er . . .

SPARKS. Just down to your pants. (*To* RUDYARD.) This shouldn't take too long, it's standard stuff. Then we can all sit down and have a chat.

RUDYARD. Good. (*To* POTTLE.) In answer to your question – a 1911, Silver Ghost.

POTTLE. Limousine?

RUDYARD. Limousine Landaulet.

POTTLE. Lovely motor car.

RUDYARD. We call her the 'Green Goblin'. What about you?

JOHN. Excuse me . . .

POTTLE. What can we do for you?

JOHN. Where shall I undress?

POTTLE. Oh, anywhere you like. Ignore us.

JOHN *does nothing*.

RUDYARD (*to* JOHN). Alright old man?

JOHN. Shall I pile my clothes on the chair?

SPARKS. Do, do.

JOHN *stands frozen, then begins very slowly to undress*.

RUDYARD. Let's give him a bit of room. We'll present a 'united back.'

RUDYARD *turns his back to* JOHN, *and moves away.*
POTTLE *follows suit.*

POTTLE. In answer to *your* question – a Napier 60.

RUDYARD. Really? That's a beautiful motor . . . Crankshaft?

POTTLE. I'm onto my third.

RUDYARD. Aaar!

POTTLE. Horrid bit of engineering.

RUDYARD. I'm afraid that's what I'd heard.

POTTLE. Presumably if you've got the 1911 Ghost – you've got the new rear axle?

RUDYARD. Absolutely – vital improvement.

SPARKS (*to* JOHN). Let's make a start young man.

RUDYARD. The new axle halves are made of steel.

POTTLE. Are they?

SPARKS *starts to examine* JOHN, *who is now naked bar his underpants. He listens to his heart.*

SPARKS. Breathe in . . .

RUDYARD. Solid steel. And they're bolted together with twenty 3/8ths of an inch diameter bolts.

SPARKS. . . . And out.

RUDYARD. What's more the torque tube is secured to the casing . . .

SPARKS. Again breathe in . . .

RUDYARD. And I still find this extraordinary,

SPARKS. And out . . .

RUDYARD. With twenty-four 3/8ths of an inch bolts.

POTTLE. Good God. I had a suspicion you were a motorist, I've just finished a story of yours.

SPARKS. Last time – in . . .

POTTLE. In which the narrator spends most of his time . . .

SPARKS. And out . . .

POTTLE. Buzzing round the Sussex countryside in a locomobile.

SPARKS (*to* RUDYARD). Oh, yes – 'Steam Tactics', that's a splendid read. (*To* JOHN.) Quick look at the ears . . . Are you keen on motor cars John?

RUDYARD. No, he's motorcycle mad, aren't you old man?

JOHN. Yes.

SPARKS. Any particular model? . . . sit down would you?

JOHN. I'd like a 'Douglas two and three quarters'.

SPARKS. Uh-huh. Cross your legs.

SPARKS *tests* JOHN*'s knee reflexes.*

My son's after a motorbike, he wants a Sidney. Other leg . . . thank you. (*To* RUDYARD.) He's just polished off the 'Jungle Books' – absolutely loved them.

RUDYARD. Oh, good . . . how are we doing?

SPARKS. Nearly there. (*To* JOHN.) On your feet. I suppose you've read all your father's stuff?

JOHN. Not really. I've never read the 'Jungle Books.'

SPARKS. I don't believe it. Well you must. Pants down please. (*To* RUDYARD.) I'm sure you're always being asked this Kipling . . . (SPARKS *cups* JOHN*'s balls in his hand.*)

Cough . . . But how on earth do you think up the stories . . . ?
Again, cough again . . .

RUDYARD. Inventing the story isn't the problem, it's putting the
jig-saw together afterwards that can be troublesome.

SPARKS (*to* JOHN). Jolly good. That's it.

RUDYARD. Clean bill of health?

SPARKS. Yes, fighting fit. Just the eye test and then we can relax.

SPARKS *flicks a switch, and a board of differently sized letters
is lit up.*

So, it's the structure that's tricky is it? Slip your togs back on . . .
I've got a surprise for you Kipling. Do you have a phonograph
at home?

RUDYARD No, I don't.

SPARKS. Splendid. Well, have a listen to this. (*Winding up the
record player.*)

POTTLE. What is it?

SPARKS. Just listen.

*The sound of thousands of men singing crackles out of the
record player. These are the words.*

'God of our fathers, known of old, Lord of our far-flung battle-
line, Beneath whose awful Hand we hold Dominion over palm
and pine – Lord God of Hosts, be with us yet, Lest we forget –
lest we forget!

'If drunk with sight of power, we loose Wild tongues that have
not thee in awe, Such boastings as the gentiles use or lesser
breeds without the law – Lord God of Hosts, be with us yet,
Lest we forget – lest we forget!'

SPARKS (*to* KIPLING). Remember this?

RUDYARD. I do indeed. How on earth did you get hold of it?

SPARKS. Aha! Exciting sound eh?

POTTLE. Wonderful, who is it?

SPARKS. It's a recording of thousands of soldiers singing
Kipling's poem 'Recessional' to the King.

POTTLE. Really?

SPARKS. I find it terribly . . . well, moving actually.

POTTLE. Yes.

SPARKS turns to JOHN and starts the eye test.

SPARKS. Right, spectacles off.

JOHN. It's a pince-nez actually.

SPARKS. Stand there. I want you to read the top line first, and work your way downwards . . . off you go.

Short silence.

JOHN. I can't see anything I'm afraid.

SPARKS. Top line, don't worry about the smaller letters for now.

The anthem finishes. Silence.

You can't read the top line?

JOHN. X? . . . T? . . . S? . . . .

SPARKS. No . . . would you walk towards the board and stop when you can clearly read the letters on the top line.

JOHN walks forward. Eventually he stops, extraordinarily close to the board.

JOHN. N – B – P – E – Q.

SPARKS. Thank you.

JOHN. Shall I try the second line?

SPARKS. No need thank you. (*He turns to* RUDYARD.) Look, I had no idea . . .

RUDYARD. What?

SPARKS. That . . . that his . . . this is very severe myopia . . . we couldn't possibly . . . (*He turns to* POTTLE *for help*.)

POTTLE. Not possibly. There are very strict guidelines.

SPARKS. I think Rory would agree, we were prepared to, um, stretch a point . . . very keen to stretch a point, but . . .

POTTLE. There has to be a limit.

SPARKS. I'm sure you understand.

RUDYARD. Yes I understand, but his spectacles are extremely effective.

SPARKS. But if he should lose them he'd be a danger to himself.

POTTLE. And to his men.

SPARKS. Indeed . . . I'm very sorry.

RUDYARD. So am I, you haven't given the boy a chance,
I honestly believe that when you witness my son's enthusiasm
and commitment to a career in the Army, you'll change your
minds . . .

POTTLE. We don't doubt his commitment.

SPARKS. Far from it.

RUDYARD. This is a very minor hiccup. I think, if only out of
respect for John, we should all sit down, and calmly and
objectively, talk this through.

SPARKS. By all means, by all means. But I have to say –
categorically – that under no circumstances could the Army
ever recruit a boy with such poor eyesight.

A tense silence.

RUDYARD. Well if it's cut and dry, if it's a fait accompli, I don't
see the point in discussing it any further.

SPARKS. Ah . . . perhaps not.

RUDYARD. I've no desire to mull it over if a decision's already
been made.

SPARKS. I am sorry.

RUDYARD. What a pity.

POTTLE. I wish I could see a way . . . um . . .

RUDYARD. I think you're making a mistake. It's a missed
opportunity. It's precisely the sort of inflexibility that this
country needs to get out of its system. John has so much to
offer. It's a great shame.

SPARKS. I agree. I do agree.

RUDYARD. Well clearly you don't . . . or we'd be looking for a
way forward . . .

He waits for a response, but doesn't get one.

Nothing you can do? . . . mmm?

SPARKS. Not that I can see.

RUDYARD. Well I'm not calling it a day. I shall write, I think it's
utterly gutless. John, come on, we're off . . . so spineless.

POTTLE. I am sorry. (RUDYARD *briskly shakes hands with*
SPARKS *and* POTTLE.)

RUDYARD. Thank you for your time . . . John?

> RUDYARD *bundles* JOHN *out of the room.* SPARKS, *and* POTTLE *remain. A moment of sheepishness, then.*

POTTLE. Awkward.

SPARKS. Yes.

POTTLE. Nothing we could do.

SPARKS. No. Do you think he will write?

POTTLE. Not our concern. One has to draw the line somewhere.

SPARKS. Precisely.

> *Blackout.*

> *End of Scene Two.*

ACT ONE SCENE THREE

September 1913. Drawing Room. Batemans.

The same day. Late at night. One small lamp is lit. JOHN *enters.*

JOHN. Awful. Horrible, horrible day . . . Hate this room.

> *He walks over to a bookshelf, lifts out a book and extricates a packet of cigarettes. He looks back at the door, listens for any sound, and then lights it.*

(*Imitating* RUDYARD.) 'Buck up old man, buck up old boy. On your side, you know that . . . '

> *He sits on the floor, resting against the back of a chair. After a short silence, a girl's voice seems to come from the chair itself.*

ELSIE'S VOICE. I want to know what the crocodile has for dinner! (*No response.*) Go to the banks of the great grey-green greasy Limpopo River all set about with fever trees and find out, O best beloved.

JOHN. Bird . . .

ELSIE'S VOICE. Good-bye. I am going to the great grey-green greasy Limpopo River, all set about with fever trees, to find out what the crocodile has for dinner.

JOHN. I didn't know you were there.

ELSIE'S VOICE. He went from . . .

BOTH . . . Graham's town to kimber-lee, From Kimberley to Khama, East by north, Eating melons all the time, Precisely as the Kolokolo bird had said.

> ELSIE KIPLING*'s face appears above the back of the chair against which* JOHN *is leaning. She looks down at her brother.*

ELSIE. O best beloved brother.

JOHN. You kept very quiet.

ELSIE. I didn't feel I should be here.

JOHN. They turned me down.

ELSIE. I know.

JOHN. I suppose everybody knows.

ELSIE. Father told me.

JOHN. Was he angry?

ELSIE. No, he was upset I think.

JOHN. Oh, God. Even worse.

ELSIE. Wasn't your fault.

JOHN. It's like a great big blanket of gloom. No-one says anything.

ELSIE. I'm relieved.

JOHN. I shall enlist as a private soldier. They can't stop me.

ELSIE. Don't be silly.

JOHN. I'm going to join the Army, I don't care how I do it.

ELSIE. I don't think it would suit you.

JOHN. Don't you? You all think you know me off by heart, and you don't.

> JOHN *spots a vase of flowers on the cabinet underneath the girl's portrait.*

Where did these come from?

ELSIE. I picked them.

JOHN. They're nice . . . don't you hate this room? It's so dark.

ELSIE. The whole house is dark.

JOHN. There's not one comfortable chair in the whole bloody building.

ELSIE. Funny thing to say.

JOHN. Not really. It's all part and parcel.

ELSIE. True though.

JOHN. It is, isn't it?

ELSIE. You shouldn't be smoking.

JOHN. I know.

ELSIE. Can I have a puff?

JOHN *hands her the cigarette.*

JOHN. Do you ever long to . . .

ELSIE. What?

JOHN. No.

ELSIE. What?

JOHN. Doesn't matter.

ELSIE. Say it.

JOHN. . . . Be someone else for a while. Or, rather, be yourself for a while, that's what I really mean. Sounds like the opposite, but in fact it's the same thing.

ELSIE. I'm not with you.

JOHN. No . . . shall we have a drink?

ELSIE. Alright.

JOHN. Whisky?

ELSIE. Why not?

JOHN. You should have seen them, it was awful.

ELSIE. Was it?

JOHN. Embarrassing.

ELSIE. Did you just fail the eye test?

JOHN. Don't know.

ELSIE. The rules are there for a reason.

JOHN. Please don't . . .

ELSIE. It seems sensible to me . . .

JOHN (*furious*). Oh, shut up. I don't care whether it's sensible or not, or dangerous or not, I don't give a damn as long as I get away, and get out of this house.

ELSIE. Ssh . . . Jack . . .

JOHN. I can't bear it.

ELSIE. Jack.

JOHN. I hate it. You don't understand.

ELSIE. I do.

JOHN. No you don't. Sometimes it makes me ill. It does. I get so upset, I actually feel sick. And I can't breathe in. I can't make myself take a breath. It's suffocating. I walk round this room . . .

ELSIE. Yes?

JOHN. He thinks I'm dim.

ELSIE. Father?

JOHN. I can't bear being 'geed up' and encouraged. I'll do it myself. Without his help. I'll enlist.

ELSIE There's no hurry.

JOHN. There is! You see, you don't understand. It has to be soon, now. I have to be with other people.

ELSIE. Oh, thank you.

JOHN. No, no, no. Not you. I don't want to leave you. I just want . . . to be myself. That's all.

ELSIE You don't have to join the Army to do that.

JOHN. No but that's what's on offer. Let's stop now. It's boring.

ELSIE. No, it isn't.

JOHN. Yes it is. Do you still want a whisky?

ELSIE. Yes I do. Hurry up.

JOHN (*organising drinks*). Did you know Josie would have been twenty-one next Wednesday?

ELSIE. I did yes.

JOHN. *I* didn't . . . I was amazed.

ELSIE. I never imagine her aging. She's always seven years old. But she's always older than me. Funny.

JOHN. I can't remember her at all.

ELSIE. Can't you?

JOHN. No . . . (*Pointing at the portrait*.) That's Josephine to
me . . . the picture . . . do you remember her well?

ELSIE. Pretty well.

JOHN. What was she like?

ELSIE. The 'grown-ups' loved her. She was ever so charming and
pretty – and she always got her way.

JOHN. Did she?

ELSIE. Father's favourite. Favourite girl anyway. You were the
boy of course, which was different.

JOHN. Was it?

ELSIE. The only son. He worshipped you.

JOHN. Where did you fit in?

ELSIE. I didn't.

JOHN. That's not true.

ELSIE. It is . . . I don't mind . . . I don't.

JOHN (*handing* ELSIE *her drink*). What shall we drink to?

ELSIE. Us?

JOHN. Best beloved sister.

ELSIE. Best beloved brother . . . don't you dare leave me alone . . .
alright?

No response.

Promise me you won't.

JOHN. What did you do today?

ELSIE. Played golf.

JOHN. Did you? Birdies and bogies n'

ELSIE. Eagles, n'

JOHN. Niblicks and Brassies n'

ELSIE. Spoons.

JOHN. Etcetera

BOTH Etcetera, etcetera.

JOHN. I'll tell you something that's difficult.

ELSIE What?

JOHN. 'Daddo' – not him – the word – 'Daddo'. I'm sixteen.

ELSIE. Nearly.

JOHN. Very nearly. I should have moved on to 'Father' by now.

ELSIE. That's up to you.

JOHN. I know but I can't quite say it.

ELSIE. Or 'Papa'.

JOHN. 'Pater!'

ELSIE. 'Pops!' . . . Ssssshhh. (*They hear creaking on the stairs.*) Quick! (*They hide the cigarette and drinks.*) Don't say anything Jack, tell them I've gone to bed. (*She leaps back into her chair.*)

RUDYARD (*offstage*). Elsie? (*He enters.*) Bird? Jack you should be in bed.

JOHN. I'm just going.

RUDYARD. It's very dark in here.

JOHN. I suppose it is.

RUDYARD. Seen Elsie?

JOHN. She's gone to bed.

RUDYARD. Ah . . . (*Silence.*) . . . Well, no need to be despondent about today.

JOHN. I'm not.

RUDYARD. Good. (*Pause.*) You must . . . buck up and look forwards.

JOHN. Yes.

RUDYARD. So . . . (*Clumsily embraces* JOHN.) . . . Hold on old man.

JOHN. I've decided to enlist as a private soldier.

RUDYARD. Well, hold your horses . . .

JOHN. No, I've decided Daddo.

RUDYARD. Don't . . . don't jump the gun – there are other avenues we can explore. There's no hurry. Alright? Let me look into it.

JOHN *nods. They stand, saying nothing for a moment.*

RUDYARD. Would you like me to stay up? . . . We could chat.

JOHN. No, it's alright, I'm going to bed in a minute.

Silence.

RUDYARD. I was so angry. So angry. They don't look beyond their noses. Rules, rules, rules, Best Beloved.

Short silence.

I'm thrilled you're so keen. And terribly proud. We'll get there.

He goes to the door, then turns to JOHN.

Bless you.

Again JOHN *nods but says nothing.*

'Night.

JOHN. 'Night.

RUDYARD *leaves.* ELSIE *pokes her head out again.*

ELSIE. Very solemn.

The door clicks open again. ELSIE *ducks down. –* RUDYARD*'s voice through the door.*

RUDYARD. You will put out that cigarette before you go up won't you.

As the door shuts again –

Blackout.

End of Scene Three.

ACT ONE SCENE FOUR

Ten months later. October 1914. The First World War is six weeks old. RUDYARD *is recruiting at a mass meeting.*

RUDYARD. Ladies and Gentlemen. We are a people who have never known invasion, have never known the shame of seeing a foreign army on our soil. A people whose soul is as strong and as old as the English oak, and as constant as the brook that cuts deep into the soft valley soil.

The German Army has reached the coast of Belgium. Fifty miles from where you sit now. If the Teuton invades our shores our English soul will be squashed and squeezed until it cries out in pain. The German will bring in his wake, riot, and arson, and disorder, and starvation, and bloodshed. The blood of our mothers, our fathers, our wives, our sons and our daughters will drench the streets of our cities, and paint our rivers red.

And after the war is over, after the riots in London and Manchester and Liverpool are quelled, when the ashes of our burnt down homes are cold, when our raped women are huddled and still . . . what then?

From across the channel, like the germs of a disease, a vile and meddlesome tribe of bureaucrats will slip unnoticed into our midst, contaminating our blood, and infecting the very body politic. They will teach our bricklayers to lay bricks the German way. They will instruct our farmers to use larger fields and cut down the hedges. They will tell us what to eat and how to eat it, what to mine and how to mine it, what to say and when to say it. Our towns will be re-named, and every book, newspaper, map, and signpost will be written in German first, English second. And in your corner shop when you buy your ounce of German tobacco, you will pay, not in pounds, shillings, and pence, but in German marks. And yet this government still supports a system of voluntary service. They believe that in this hour of danger there will always be enough men willing to defend their country.

But there is of course a pernicious minority who do not intend to inconvenience themselves for any consideration.

We must demand that every fit young man come forward to enlist. And that every young man who chooses to remain at home, be shunned by his community.

Only our unity, our strength, and our courage can save us from destruction.

End of Scene Four.

ACT ONE SCENE FIVE

October 1914. Two weeks later. Drawing room. Batemans.

On and off one can hear, faintly, the sound of the guns in France.
RUDYARD *stands at the window, looking out expectantly.*
CARRIE *is cataloguing books.* ELSIE *is agitated.*

ELSIE. I'd like to know WHY?

CARRIE (*to* RUDYARD). Any sign?

RUDYARD. Not yet, no.

ELSIE. I've been away for three weeks, I come home, and my brother's in the Army. Why have they changed their mind?

RUDYARD. Regarding what Bird?

ELSIE (*impatiently*). Jack's eyesight!

RUDYARD. Oh. I don't know.

ELSIE. Of course you know (*No response from* RUDYARD.) . . . Father?

RUDYARD. We're at war. Criteria change.

ELSIE. Not that quickly. It's only been going a month.

RUDYARD. Well anyway. This isn't the moment.

ELSIE. Three times the Army has turned Jack down. Why is he suddenly fit to fight?

CARRIE (*to* RUDYARD). What's the time?

RUDYARD. It's after half past.

ELSIE. Don't ignore me!

RUDYARD (*to* CARRIE). He should be here by now.

ELSIE He can't see five yards without his specs. Doesn't it worry you that he may be killed?

RUDYARD. That is not the issue.

CARRIE (*quietly*). It is absolutely the issue, of course we are concerned.

RUDYARD. As are thousands of families. We're all in the same boat.

ELSIE. It's nothing to do with boats. What a silly phrase that is.

RUDYARD. Elsie if you can't be civil, go away.

CARRIE (*very tense. Holding up a book to* RUDYARD.) This hasn't a name plate Rud.

RUDYARD. Hasn't it?

CARRIE. It's covered in dust. I'm not even sure it should be in this room. Where do you house Longfellow?

RUDYARD. In my study.

CARRIE. As I thought.

ELSIE. Mother.

CARRIE. It's simply not good enough. I try to maintain a
scrupulously catalogued library. This book is filthy! Filthy!

ELSIE. Mother!

CARRIE (*to* ELSIE). I'm talking. (*To* RUDYARD.) She's a
professional secretary. Surely Miss Howard must see how
important it is that every single book in your collection is
properly listed . . .

ELSIE. MOTHER!

CARRIE. So that you can refer to it at a moment's notice.

RUDYARD. I'm sure there's a reason.

CARRIE. No, it's slovenly and inefficient. This sort of error must
not occur.

RUDYARD (*seeing* JOHN *arrive*). He's here! He's here!

CARRIE. Is he? (*She looks out of the window.*) There he is . . .
(*She calls out.*) Jack!

ELSIE Good, I'm glad he's arrived, I shall ask Jack.

RUDYARD. Don't. Please. Bird don't.

ELSIE. Why shouldn't I?

RUDYARD. Don't spoil it. Don't spoil it for everyone.

RUDYARD *leaves the room.*

CARRIE. Do I look respectable?

ELSIE. It's so senseless.

CARRIE. How do I look?

ELSIE. It's only Jack. It's not the king.

CARRIE (*grabbing* ELSIE*'s arm and confronting her*). Elsie. I am
terrified that Jack will be killed. I dream of his death – night
after night. Two of his friends are dead already. But there is
nothing I can do about it. So, please . . .

RUDYARD (*offstage*). Come on through old man. Everyone's
here.

CARRIE (*to* ELSIE). Let him be.

> RUDYARD *and* JOHN *enter.* JOHN *is smiling broadly. He has grown a moustache and looks much older. He is in full uniform.*

RUDYARD. Here he is.

JOHN. Hello everyone.

CARRIE (*racing over to greet him. She flings her arms around his neck*). Hello! You look exhausted.

JOHN. It's been a thick week. Hello Bird.

ELSIE. You've grown a moustache.

JOHN. Do you like it?

ELSIE. You look ten years older.

JOHN. Is that a good thing?

ELSIE. Of course . . . so . . . What are you?

JOHN. 2nd Lieutenant John Kipling, Irish Guards, Brigade of Guards, 2nd reserve batallion.

ELSIE. You got what you wanted.

CARRIE (*still holding* JACK). You look so fine.

RUDYARD (*firmly disentangling* CARRIE *from her son*). Come on give everybody a chance. How are you old man?

JOHN. Fatigued. We've had four hours sleep this last forty-eight hours.

CARRIE. Poor you.

RUDYARD. Lot of marching?

JOHN. Absolutely.

ELSIE. Jack, no-one will tell me why the Army have had a change of heart.

RUDYARD (*furious*). Not now!

ELSIE. Yes, now.

JOHN. I don't mind Father.

RUDYARD. I *do* mind. Go on old man.

JOHN. Well . . . we did nineteen miles on Tuesday, it was filthy hot, the men were fainting like flies . . .

RUDYARD. Do you think they'll stick it?

JOHN. Oh yes, they're good men. 100 per cent Irish and 100 per cent mad, but they'll stick it! Then last night we marched twenty miles. We started at nine p.m. and weren't in 'til six this morning.

RUDYARD. Allah be praised.

ELSIE. You don't mind being tired do you Jack? You're probably too happy to care . . . I want to know why they changed their mind.

RUDYARD. This is so selfish.

JOHN. It's no great secret Bird.

ELSIE. Good, you can tell me then.

JOHN. You know 'Bobs'?

ELSIE. No.

JOHN. Yes you do. Lord Roberts.

ELSIE. *The* Lord Roberts? Father's pal?

JOHN. He helped us out . . . he found me a space in his regiment.

ELSIE. But he's dead isn't he?

Silence.

Isn't he?

JOHN. He'd been ill for some time . . .

ELSIE. So he *is* dead?

RUDYARD. 'Bobs' forced the pace a bit that's all. It was typically generous, at a time when he was very groggy.

ELSIE. I'll say.

RUDYARD. He was a great friend, a great soldier, and Jack and I are immensely grateful.

ELSIE. When did he die?

RUDYARD. This is not constructive.

ELSIE. When did he die?

JOHN. . . . About a week ago I think . . .

ELSIE. Phew! A close run thing, you got to him just in time.

RUDYARD. *Enough*.

ELSIE. That's dreadful! Father that's awful! You march up to one of your powerful pals, who's on the point of conking out, and . . .

JOHN. Leave it 'Bird'.

ELSIE. No I won't, it's appalling. He's not likely to argue the toss on his deathbed is he?

RUDYARD. That's enough!

ELSIE (*furious*). What was the point of those examinations? All totally humiliating for you Jack, and they all said the same thing – your eyesight isn't good enough. It's too dangerous. Well frankly Father it'll be your fault if Jack is killed.

RUDYARD. Get out!

ELSIE. No I won't.

RUDYARD. GET OUT!

ELSIE. Mother, didn't you try to stop him?

CARRIE. Yes, I did.

ELSIE. You did? But the men ploughed on regardless did they?

RUDYARD. This is intolerable.

ELSIE (*to* RUDYARD). Why did you do it?

RUDYARD (*passionately*). You don't *understand* . . . neither of you understand what is at stake.

ELSIE. Yes we do.

RUDYARD. I don't think so. What our country has achieved in the last 150 years is unique. We have built up, painstakingly built up, a family of nations . . .

ELSIE. Oh, please Father.

RUDYARD. Listen to me! A family of nations. And Britain, as parents – Mother and Father, has an absolute duty to protect its children, and some of the children are self-sufficient young adults, and need only a nudge in one direction or the other. But some are still bawling, inarticulate, aggressive kids, who need all the help and direction we can offer. But it *is* a family. And it is our responsibility as parents to feed, to educate, to guide, to maintain our children's quality of life.

ELSIE. And to make money.

RUDYARD. Of course! That's absolutely right. That's why our
empire is uniquely successful. We have managed to combine
benevolence and commerce. No-one has done it before. Not
only are our children better off spiritually but they are better
off materially. From Canada to Australia, from Africa to India,
the world is a better place, a safer place, a more comfortable
place than it was a hundred years ago.

ELSIE. And to preserve that you would put your son's life at risk?

RUDYARD. Not worthy of you . . .

ELSIE. That's the equation isn't it?

RUDYARD. No it isn't.

ELSIE. You don't think for one second that Jack gives a damn
about the British Empire – do you?

JOHN. I do give a damn.

ELSIE. No you don't. You've said you don't.

JOHN. I have not.

ELSIE (*to* RUDYARD *and* CARRIE). Have you actually stopped
to wonder why he's so keen to get to France? . . . Have you?

RUDYARD I don't know what you're talking about.

ELSIE. No, you don't, you absolutely don't. But I can promise
you, it is nothing to do with Great Britain, or the Empire, or
the Germans, or anything half so honourable . . .

Silence.

(*To* JOHN.) It'd be a funny sort of freedom if anything
happened to you wouldn't it?

RUDYARD (*very quietly*). There is a price we have to pay. There
is a risk we all have to take. Jack knows that. Germany will go
on killing by all the means in its power. She must either win
or bleed to death. Therefore we must continue to pass our
children through fire, until somehow *we* win and destroy her.

ELSIE (*suddenly quiet and forlorn*). Haven't we had our share as
a family? Haven't we?

CARRIE (*looking out of the window, she notices someone on the
lawn*). Who is that? There's someone on the lawn. (*Shouting*.)
This is a private garden! For God's sake, there's an intruder in
the garden. (*Shouting again*.) This is not a zoo! We are not
animals in a zoo. (*Turning round to the family*.) Why on earth

do they feel they have the right to gawp at us, tramp over the gardens, with their Kodaks click clicking away.

ELSIE (*touches her mother's arm*). Mother . . .

CARRIE (*jumping away as if electrocuted*). Don't. Please don't. Nothing makes me angrier you know that. (*She looks out again.*) He's damn well seen us, he's coming this way. (*Shouting.*) Get out! This is a private garden. Get off our land!

RUDYARD. Calmly.

CARRIE. I won't have it. (*She suddenly slams the window shut, closes all the curtains, and turns round with her back to the windows.*) Don't stare at me all of you.

ELSIE. We're not.

CARRIE. Yes you are . . . John? (*She looks at him desperately.*)

JOHN. Yes?

CARRIE. Jack . . . (*She trails off. She turns and peeks between the curtains.*) He's still there. Right! Bird come with me.

CARRIE *leaves*. ELSIE *doesn't follow immediately.*
RUDYARD *opens the curtains.*

JOHN. I shall need your permission Father, to go out as soon as I'm eighteen.

RUDYARD. Of course.

ELSIE. Of course. What a shame we can't get you out there sooner.

She follows her Mother out of the room. Silence.

JOHN. Sixteen chaps from Warley barracks have been killed already . . . George, Oscar, . . . and forty-two wounded . . . frightening . . . a bit.

RUDYARD. Of course it is.

JOHN. I wonder if I will die?

RUDYARD. I don't think so.

JOHN. Why not?

RUDYARD (*touching JACK's forehead*). You'll be alright.

JOHN. When I'm busy I don't think about it at all. But sometimes at night . . . I wonder about George and Oscar . . . what it felt like . . . how much it hurt . . . whether they mind now.

RUDYARD. You're facing a . . . loneliness of the spirit which I know is awfully hard to bear. Would it help you to know I had to face something of the same sort?

JOHN. Did you?

RUDYARD. Before I married, I lived in the pocket of my true friend, Woolcot. We ate together, we jawed together – about everything, we even wrote together, and then he upped and died of Typhoid. He was twenty-seven, and I was very fond of him. And for a long while I had the general feeling that the world was a wicked place. But you have to take your dose.

JOHN. Do you?

RUDYARD. You sit it out. You wait. Eventually you heal up. I'll tell you something old man, I wish I could be in your shoes now. I wish that I could share with you that clean, honourable task which is ahead of you.

JOHN. It *is* an honourable task . . . isn't it? The sooner I get out there the better. (RUDYARD *places a hand on* JOHN*'s shoulder*.)

End of Scene Five.

ACT ONE SCENE SIX

The Western Front. France. September. 1915.

It is raining heavily. An Irish Soldier, Guardsman McHUGH, *sits huddled under his oilskin. Beside him are his helmet and his rifle.*

For a moment, just the sound of rain, then an enormous explosion rocks the trench. McHUGH *leaps to his feet.*

McHUGH. Fuck. Fuck. Jesus Christ.

He grabs his helmet and rifle, and runs to the side of the stage. He looks off. Then he returns and climbs a few rungs of the ladder leaning against the trench wall. He balances the helmet on the barrel of his rifle, reaches up, and pokes it over the top of the trench. A moment. It isn't shot at. Reassured, he lowers the helmet, puts it on, climbs two or three more rungs and peeps over the top. Nothing there. No attack imminent. He climbs down and sits with an air of studied calm.

Two more Irish soldiers, Guardsmen DOYLE *and* BOWE, *run on carrying spades.*

DOYLE. McHugh, you are a parasitical bastard.

McHUGH. Have yous dug your latrine?

DOYLE. Are yous allergic to work?

McHUGH. Would the latrine be ready for use now?

DOYLE. Where were yous?

McHUGH. I regret not bein' there Doyle, but I'm after sufferin' serious stomach cramps.

DOYLE. No you're not, you're an un-carin', selfish, city bastard, an' when Jerry blows your head off, I won't feel an ounce o' pity.

McHUGH. I was more than willin' to help yous – unfortunately I've got the cramps, on account o' needin' a shit.

DOYLE. Jesus.

McHUGH. So I'll ask yous again, have yous dug the latrine? Because if yous have . . .

BOWE. The shell hit the fuckin' latrine. It's the biggest fuckin' latrine in France, room for the whole platoon to have a dump together . . . Listen McHugh, on the farm at home, I'm up at four every mornin', of every day, of every year, an' if I'm not in the pink o' health miself, I can't complain to the cows can I?

McHUGH. No, you've lost me there Bowe.

BOWE. We dug a beautiful hole, an' Corporal Donovan was after fillin' it wi' bromide o' lime, we seen 'im, fillin' it, casual like, an' the shell landed, blown to fuckin' pieces he was – lime everywhere.

Another shell explodes. Much closer this time. All three men duck.

BOWE. Mother o' Jesus shelter me.

DOYLE. Fuckin' Jesus.

McHUGH *leaps onto the lower rungs of the ladder again, he listens intently. Off stage, getting louder and nearer, an officer can be heard shouting: 'Feet, feet!'*

McHUGH. Not now. For God's sake not now you asshole.

BOWE (*frightened*). In County Clare they're havin' the finest harvest for one hundred years.

BOWE *starts to pull off his boots and socks. The cries of 'Feet, feet' get closer.*

That's where I should be, in the fields, with a dung fork in mi hand an' the sun on mi back.

DOYLE *warily undoes the lace of one boot.* McHUGH *does nothing.*

McHUGH. I would rather go over the top and face a hundred Maxim machine guns than examine your feet three times a week, Doyle.

DOYLE. My feet are delightful, I only wish they weren't. I want a lasting case o' trench foot, I want my feet to rot, I want the gangrene to set in, an' then they'll be after whiskin' me away from here, to a nice, warm, dry, hospital bed.

BOWE. In County Clare, on the farm . . .

McHUGH. Jesus, will you fuck off with your soddin' rural idyll! Do yous know, you might find this extraordinary, but I don't want to hear how the farmers of Clare look after their feet.

JOHN *enters, laden with tins of whale grease and talcum powder.*

JOHN. Feet! . . . Whale grease. Talcum powder.

JOHN *places a tin of grease and a tin of talcum powder in front of the soldiers.*

BOWE. Is it an attack sir?

JOHN. No, it is not.

BOWE. They hit the latrine sir.

JOHN. One shell is not an attack Bowe.

BOWE. Two sir.

JOHN. It is not an attack. McHugh, Doyle, feet.

McHUGH *ignores him,* DOYLE *responds.*

McHugh take your boots off please.

McHUGH *does nothing.* JOHN *carries on across the stage and off the other side. His shouts of 'Feet' recede down the line.*

DOYLE (*to* McHUGH). What's he done to you?

McHUGH *says nothing.*

What's he done to you for fuck's sake?

BOWE (*holding a bare foot up to* DOYLE). Will you powder me?

DOYLE (*re.* BOWE'*s feet*). Bring them here then.

BOWE. You don't think it's the start of an attack then Doyle?

DOYLE *gently rubs* BOWE'*s feet and starts to powder them*.

BOWE (*ecstatic*). Oh, that feels so good . . . Yes . . . Oh thass lovely . . . thass better.

McHUGH. Jesus, I've just had a terrible image of you in bed with your wife Bowe. I feel sick.

BOWE. Make sure yous do between the toes . . . Not an attack then?

DOYLE *parts* BOWE'*s toes. This produces a scream of pain from* BOWE.

OUCH! Jesus, what are yous doin'? God almighty are yous after tearin' my toes off?

BOWE *pulls his foot away*.

DOYLE. Yous wanted me to do between the toes. Come here. Bring it back here . . . bring it here!

BOWE. Be gentle with me.

DOYLE. I am for fuck's sake, jus' gimme your foot.

McHUGH. You're a sadist Doyle.

DOYLE. I hardly touched 'im. Gimme your foot Bowe.

BOWE. Jus' be gentle will yous.

BOWE *gingerly presents his foot again*.

Please be careful . . . Mother o' Jesus, ow, ow, ow . . .

DOYLE. You poor sod, you've got a crack here the size of a valley.

JOHN *is back, having handed out all the grease and powder*.

BOWE. Ow, ow, Jesus you're hurtin' . . .

DOYLE (*examining the crack*). An' it's sort o' yellow, yellowish green, with a kind o' pink fringe.

JOHN. Nice of you to put us in the picture Doyle.

DOYLE. Look at this sir.

JOHN *kneels and places* BOWE's *foot on his lap*.

JOHN. That must hurt.

BOWE. It does sir. Is it the trench foot?

JOHN. I don't think so. The foot's a good colour. Any numbness?

BOWE. No, I can feel it alright sir.

JOHN. Pass me the powder.

DOYLE *does so.*

You must get foot rot in the winter, on the farm?

BOWE. Not if you dry them off at the end o' the day.

JOHN. McHugh, I asked you to take off your boots.

McHUGH *does nothing, says nothing.*

(*To* BOWE.) Hold still. You must hold still.

JOHN *prises the offending toes apart. He pours on the powder.*

BOWE. Ow, ow, ow.

JOHN. How many spare pairs of socks do you have?

BOWE. Only the one, an' they're soakin' wet.

JOHN. I'll try and find you a dry pair. Doyle, I want you to look after Bowe's feet.

DOYLE. Do I have to sir?

JOHN. I want him to powder twice a day, and put on a dry pair of socks twice a day.

DOYLE. Yes sir.

JOHN. And if he develops gangrene or trench foot, I shall hold you personally responsible, and have you up before the battalion commander . . . understood?

DOYLE. Yes sir.

JOHN. This will be the last inspection for some time . . . We're going over this afternoon. It's the great effort to break through and end the war. Our first action. Our first shell-fire in the open. So. Feet in good working order. McHugh, I'd like you to take your boots off. And if there's a reason you won't, I'd like you to tell me what it is.

McHUGH *says nothing, does nothing.*

McHugh?

Silence.

Before we risk our lives together, I'd like you to explain why you grab any chance to disobey me.

Silence.

I'm going to fetch Bowe a dry pair of socks, and when I come back, I'd like to see your feet.

JOHN *leaves.* McHUGH *removes his boots and socks.*

McHUGH. What a stupid fuckin' time to be after checkin' the state of our feet. D'yous know, there are three British protestant bastards that my brother Sean would murder without compunction, and top of his list is Rudyard Kipling. And do you know something Doyle, I would hold his arm steady as he aimed the rifle . . . so don't you find it a little fuckin' ironic that here we are, in a platoon of Irish catholics, takin' orders from the son of a man who gave £30,000 of his own cash, to help Mr. Carson arm the protestants. Don't you think that's a little ironical?

BOWE. Jesus, has it gone cold suddenly? I can't stop the shiverin'.

DOYLE. Don't land us in the shit McHugh.

BOWE. Do you think it's true? We go over today? D'you know I wasn't scared till that exact second. When the lieutenant was after talkin' about goin' over. Jesus I'm cold. Are yous cold?

McHUGH *has started smearing something onto his feet.*

DOYLE. What the fuck are you doin'?

McHUGH. Jus' livenin' things up for the lieutenant.

DOYLE. What is it?

McHUGH. Horse shit.

DOYLE. Bastard.

JOHN *returns carrying a pair of socks.*

JOHN. There you are.

He arrives at McHUGH's *feet.*

McHUGH. There you go sir.

McHUGH *places a stinking foot in* JOHN's *hand. After a moment's massage* JOHN *takes his hands away and looks at them. They are covered in horse shit.* JOHN *struggles to keep his temper.*

JOHN. McHugh . . . I'm trying . . . I'm trying . . . Isn't it funny how a smell can take you back . . . I was very keen on horse riding. (*He holds up his hands*.) This takes me straight back to weekends at the stables in Hawkhurst . . . Your feet are fine McHugh. Put your socks and boots back on, could I just . . . (*He leans over and grabs a bit of* McHUGH*'s jacket. He wipes his hands on it.*) . . . Thank you.

JOHN *lets go of* McHUGH. *Silence.*

Wouldn't it be awful nice if this rain stopped for a moment . . . have any of you got a dry handkerchief about you?

DOYLE. Actually I have sir . . . there's only one place on the whole body that stays entirely dry, do you know where that is?

JOHN. I hate to think.

DOYLE. The top o' the head.

He lifts off his tin helmet to reveal a gleaming white handkerchief.

There you are sir.

JOHN. Thank you.

He takes the handkerchief, and dries his spectacles.

You can't win. If I take them off, I'm blind as a bat, if I keep them on, it's like looking through a rainy window . . .

BOWE. In County Clare sir, they're after experiencin' the driest autumn for over a hundred years.

JOHN. Of course they are – there's no rain left. The Irish Guards have brought it all to France.

End of Scene Six.

ACT ONE SCENE SEVEN

France. September 1915.

A few hours later. Half an hour to 'Zero Hour'. BOWE, McHUGH, *and* DOYLE *are waiting for* JOHN *to arrive with tots of rum. Three plates of untouched food sit on the stage in front of the soldiers. It is still raining heavily.*

McHUGH. Where's the soddin' anaesthetic?

BOWE (*shivering uncontrollably*). Jesus I'm freezin'.

McHUGH. Where's the Lieutenant and the booze?

BOWE. I think it's a fever, freezin' one minute, an' hot the next.

McHUGH. They want us pissed Doyle . . . they want to kill off any thoughts o' death eatin' away at our minds.

DOYLE. Will yous shut your mouth.

McHUGH. Weakenin' our resolve, remindin' us that half of us will be fuckin' deceased by this evenin' . . .

DOYLE. Jus' shut your mouth will ya. Shut . . . your . . . evil . . . mouth . . . Merciful Jesus . . . Yous are unbelievable!

BOWE (*on the edge*). I can't stop the shiverin'. It starts in the cheeks an' creeps all the way down to the feet. Have yous ever had that McHugh? . . . I think it's the fever you know . . . I need to find somewhere warm. Mother o' God France is s'posed to be a hotter, drier place, isn't it, an' it's ice cold, an' we're soaked to the skin.

DOYLE. When d'you think we'll go over?

McHUGH. Not long, if they're after gettin' us pissed now.

As if on cue, the noise of the bombardment prior to the attack, suddenly increases. The sound of the shells should get gradually, but relentlessly, louder through this scene and the next.

McHUGH (*re. noise*). Fuck!

DOYLE. Shit!

There is a huge explosion.

BOWE. Jesus, what was that?

McHUGH. Fifteen inch!

DOYLE. Must a' been – fifteen inch!

BOWE. Oh, God, if I could jus' stop the shakin' . . . Where d'yous think I can find somewhere warm . . . an' out o' the noise. I need to warm up for God's sake . . . , I'm after tremblin' like a leaf. I think I'll jus' make my way back to the dug-out . . . jus' for a moment, jus' to thaw out you know . . . 'scuse me lads, d'you think I could jus' get past yous . . .

BOWE tries ever so politely, and on the surface, calmly, to pass McHUGH and DOYLE, in order to get out of the front line.

McHUGH. Where the fuck do yous think you're goin'?

BOWE. I jus' need to warm up a bit, so I thought I might nip back to the dug-out, jus for a moment.

DOYLE. Fuck off Bowe!

McHUGH. You're not goin' anywhere.

BOWE. Lads, if you could . . . 'scuse me . . . could you get out o' the way please . . .

BOWE *is beginning to panic. He tries to barge past* McHUGH *and* DOYLE.

McHUGH (*grabbing* BOWE *and pushing him back*). I'll kill yous first.

BOWE. I need to get past . . .

McHUGH. I said, you're not goin' anywhere.

BOWE. PLEASE.

McHUGH. Doyle! Give us a hand.

BOWE (*desperate*). I need another coat or somethin' . . .

McHUGH. I'm not havin' yous put a fuckin' curse on this platoon.

BOWE. Could yous get out o' my way!

McHUGH. Doyle grab him!

BOWE (*shouting*). GET OUT O' MY WAY. LET ME PAST!

BOWE *'claws' at* DOYLE.

DOYLE. Don't yous fuckin' scratch me . . .

BOWE. I'm sick, you've got to let me through . . .

DOYLE. Don't you scratch me – you bastard . . .

BOWE. Let – me – through!

McHUGH. Fuck you!

McHUGH *hits* BOWE *hard in the face.* BOWE *reels back against the trench wall. At the same moment,* JOHN *appears with the rum rations. It is unclear whether he has witnessed the incident. He stops by* McHUGH. BOWE *is hunched, nursing his injury.*

JOHN. McHugh you're not eating.

McHUGH. No sir.

JOHN. I think you should.

McHUGH. No thankyou sir.

JOHN. Rum?

McHUGH. Thankyou sir.

JOHN (*arriving at* DOYLE'*s untouched food*). None of you have eaten.

DOYLE. It's a precaution sir. We don't want to be shot in the gut on a full stomach.

JOHN. I see.

McHUGH. You can imagine sir, all that poison swillin' around your insides, an' you're shot . . . here (*He indicates his stomach*.) An' your organs are open to the elements an' there's half digested food spillin' out, it's after increasin' the chances of infection.

JOHN. Yes I see.

DOYLE. You're welcome to mine if you're hungry sir.

JOHN. No thankyou . . . (*To* DOYLE.) Rum?

DOYLE. As much as you can possibly spare, and then a little more please sir.

JOHN. You'll get your share.

> JOHN *reaches* BOWE.

You're bleeding.

BOWE. Am I sir? I didn't know that.

JOHN (*enigmatic*). You'll be alright once you're on the move.

BOWE. Hope so sir.

JOHN. You will . . . rum?

BOWE. Thank you sir . . . it might help you know. It's freezin' don't you think sir?

JOHN (*staring straight at* McHUGH). I'm sure Guardsman McHugh will take care of you.

> JOHN *moves off, but before leaving, he calls* DOYLE *over to him.*

JOHN. Doyle . . . everyone alright?

DOYLE. Yes sir.

JOHN. Bowe?

DOYLE. It might be safer for all of us, if a shell fell on Bowe now . . . if you know what I mean sir.

JOHN. I think he'll be alright . . . you seem to have the situation under control, I'm sure there'll be no panic. What about this rain? Do you think it'll stop?

DOYLE (*looking at the sky*). It's not lookin' good sir.

JOHN. No it isn't, is it.

DOYLE. May I . . .

JOHN. Yes, back you go.

> DOYLE *returns to his place with* McHUGH *and* BOWE. JOHN *has learned from* DOYLE, *he lifts his cap to reveal a dry handkerchief. He dries his glasses.*

Bloody rain . . . bloody, bloody, bloody, rain.

End of Scene Seven.

ACT ONE SCENE EIGHT

France. September 1915.

It is five minutes to Zero Hour. BOWE, McHUGH, DOYLE, *and* JOHN *are about to go over the top.*

The noise of the bombardment is unbelievably loud. It is still raining.

JOHN (*holding up one hand. Shouting*). FIVE – MINUTES! Load up.

> *The soldiers start picking up their gear, which, in addition to their seventy-five pound back pack, rifle, wiring stake, Mills bomb, and shovel, includes a cage containing a live pigeon.*

McHUGH. How are yous supposed to climb out o' the trench, let alone fuckin' run.

BOWE (*he is now shaking like a leaf*). I can't . . . Jesus, I can't get the strap over. McHugh, will yous help me get the strap over . . .

McHUGH. I'm sure the Boche'll supply me with a fuckin' shovel when I get there.

BOWE. McHugh . . . someone help me get the strap over, I – can't – do – it! McHugh . . .

McHUGH. Fuck – Fuck – Fuck off Bowe!

DOYLE. (*holding up his rifle*). Shit there's mud in the barrel.

He immediately undoes his trousers and tries to urinate down the barrel.

McHUGH. Don't piss in my direction you filthy bastard.

BOWE. It's alright I've done it! Jesus, sacred heart o' Jesus, I've done it.

McHUGH. Haven't yous got enough rain to lubricate your fuckin' rifle?

DOYLE (*unable to urinate*). Shit, shit, come on, come on.

BOWE. . . . I'm so cold . . .

McHUGH. Don't piss on me Doyle!

DOYLE. Come on.

McHUGH (*screaming at* DOYLE). Don't piss on me Doyle – don't point your scabby cock at me!

BOWE. Mother o' God let me live.

DOYLE (*desperately shaking his penis*). Come on, come on, come on. Sir . . . Sir mi rifle's blocked with the mud, an' I can't piss.

JOHN (*all shouted*). Listen everyone.

DOYLE. I've been shittin' an' pissin' all day an' now I can't do it.

JOHN. Listen! When you go over you will see 'Chalk Pit Wood' five hundred yards ahead of you – advance straight for the trees. 'C' Platoon has been instructed to take pigeon baskets. It is of A-1 importance that you hold onto these until you get to the German trenches.

McHUGH. What are they for sir?

JOHN. When you reach the enemy trenches, you will release your pigeon. It will find it's way back to H.Q. and senior officers will be alerted that we have done our job.

McHUGH. Will yous look at us sir, I can't carry all this.

JOHN. You'll find a way . . . Two minutes.

The soldiers pick up their pigeon baskets. DOYLE *has given up the idea of urinating to unblock his rifle, he is now scraping at the barrel with his fingers and jerking the rifle up and down to free it.*

DOYLE. I – can't – go – yet.

McHUGH (*looking at his pigeon basket*). Fuckin' Jesus I'm goin' to be killed.

DOYLE. I – can't – go – yet.

BOWE (*sincerely panicked*). Sir! – Sir! My pigeon's dead!

JOHN. What?

BOWE. My pigeon's dead – what shall I do?

JOHN *approaches* BOWE.

JOHN. How do you know it's dead?

BOWE. It's after lyin' on the bottom of the basket – it's not movin'.

JOHN. For God's sake . . .

BOWE. Do I have to take the basket across if the pigeon's dead sir?

JOHN. If you're sure it's dead and not just . . . if you're sure it's dead, then no, of course not.

BOWE. . . . So I'll jus' dump the basket then?

JOHN. Dump the bloody . . . yes . . . shut up! Shut up! Of course dump the bloody thing.

McHUGH. You can take mine Bowe.

Suddenly the bombardment stops – completely. The silence is eerie and total. The soldiers fall silent too. DOYLE *gives up on his rifle. They stand, waiting, over-laden, like three surreal, khaki christmas trees. The seconds pass.*

JOHN *consults his watch. No longer needing to shout, he speaks quite quietly.*

JOHN. One minute.

Ten, fifteen, twenty seconds pass. Every movement is amplified and distinct. A horse whinnies, an isolated command further down the line, birds in the sky – silence again.

Fix bayonets.

Sudden activity. The sound of metal scraping, McHUGH *and* DOYLE*'s bayonets click into position.* BOWE *is shaking so much he can't do it.*

BOWE. Oh God – help me, help me someone, I can't do it, the fingers won't work.

He looks around for help but no-one is interested. He fumbles and drops the bayonet, it sinks into the mud.

Oh Jesus – sir – it's in the mud, oh no, it's lost. God help me find it. It must be here somewhere, it must be easy to find, where is it? Where is it? I can't go without it.

BOWE *scrabbles in the mud, but then gives up. He stands, strained, motionless. The seconds pass. Someone coughs. The sound of equipment moving as a soldier shifts his weight from one foot to the other. Silence.* JOHN *takes off his glasses a final time, and as he dries them, the lights close in on his face and we penetrate his thoughts.*

JOHN. I'm *so* frightened.

My heart is beating everywhere, behind my eyes, down my legs, in my chest . . . pulsing, hammering.

It's cold.

Please God I mustn't let them down. Will I be brave? Will I fail? – Onto the firestep – keep the pistol out of the mud – left hand on the parapet – pull – right foot on the sand bags – push up – left leg over – Straighten – run – I mustn't let them down. Some of these men will be dead tonight. I may be dead tonight. Let me live. Stop raining – just for a second.

Oh Daddo – what luxury – to turn on a hot water tap – hot steaming water – evening clothes – dinner at the Ritz – the Alhambra afterwards. Elsie. Mother. Daddo. – My first action – Fifteen seconds – is that the whistle? – one clear blast – left hand – parapet – sand bags – over – run. Run fast and straight. Please God let me live. Pistol high – run, run, run.

The silence is broken by twenty, thirty, whistles sounding all down the line. JOHN *looks at his watch. Zero Hour. He blows his whistle.* BOWE, DOYLE, McHUGH, *and* JOHN *climb up and over.* McHUGH *and* DOYLE *let out a long, primal, piercing scream to defy their fear. The sound cuts through the noise of the attack.*

Blackout.

End of Act One.

ACT TWO SCENE ONE

October 1st. 1915. The drawing room, Batemans.

Four days later. RUDYARD *stands, holding a small silver tray. On the tray is a telegram. He is very still. He stares at the telegram. Silence. Then.*

RUDYARD. 'It was not part of their blood
It came to them very late
With long arrears to make good
When the English began to hate!'

RUDYARD *places the tray on his desk. He picks up the telegram, and carrying it unopened, he walks round the room.*

'When the English began to hate.
It was not part of their blood . . .
When the English began to hate.
Their was neither sign nor show,
When the English began to hate . . .
It was not preached to the crowd
When the English began to hate.
When the English began to hate . . . '

RUDYARD *goes to the door and calls to* CARRIE.

Come and listen.

After a moment CARRIE *is at the door. She's busy and preoccupied.*

CARRIE. You're not ready.

RUDYARD. It's only three verses.

CARRIE. You're not even dressed.

RUDYARD. I just need you to hear them once.

CARRIE. We leave in half an hour.

RUDYARD (*an instruction*). Please listen.

CARRIE *sees the telegram.*

CARRIE (*very alarmed*). Rud . . . ?

RUDYARD. 'It was not part of their blood . . . ' Are you listening?

Short silence.

CARRIE. I shan't be any help.

RUDYARD. You will. You always are.

CARRIE doesn't reply. Her eyes are on the telegram.
RUDYARD reads the poem.

It was not part of their blood
It came to them very late
With long arrears to make good
When the English began to hate.

Their voices were even and low
Their eyes were level and straight
There was neither sign nor show,
When the English began to hate.

It was not preached to the crowd
It was not taught by the state
No man said it aloud
When the English began to hate.

CARRIE. I think, in the last verse . . .

RUDYARD. Yes?

CARRIE. 'Spoke' would be better than 'said'.

RUDYARD. No man spoke it aloud?

CARRIE. Yes.

RUDYARD. Right.

CARRIE *(frightened)*. Rud . . . ?

RUDYARD. Other than 'spoke' instead of 'said' you think it should stand?

CARRIE Is the last line too harsh?

RUDYARD. Absolutely not. That line is correct.

Short silence.

Where's Bird?

CARRIE. We thought it would be nice to take a present from John. She's in the village looking for something. Just something small.

Short silence.

Did you find a collar?

RUDYARD. Yes I did.

CARRIE. Please hurry – we'll be late.

> CARRIE *leaves.* RUDYARD *walks to the table, he makes a couple of notes. The telegram is still in his hand, unopened. Eventually* RUDYARD *puts down his pen and looks at the telegram.*

RUDYARD. Jack . . .

He opens the telegram.

No. No. No. No. No. No . . . Oh No.

He is very still.

Please, if there is a God, let Jack live. (*Shouting.*) Carrie! Carrie!

CARRIE *is at the door, frightened.*

Sit down.

CARRIE. Rud . . . ?

RUDYARD. Sit down please. (CARRIE *sits.*) John . . .

CARRIE (*a scream*). No!

RUDYARD. Is not dead.

CARRIE. What's happened?

RUDYARD. John is not *dead*.

CARRIE. Give me that.

RUDYARD. He is missing.

CARRIE. Give me that. (*Grabs the telegram.*)

RUDYARD. He is missing, believed wounded.

CARRIE. . . . Jack . . .

RUDYARD. He might not be seriously hurt.

CARRIE. . . . Jack . . .

RUDYARD. Carrie.

CARRIE. My child. My little child.

RUDYARD. He may very well have strolled into H.Q. by now. He may have got lost. That happens fairly frequently you know.

CARRIE. Two weeks, he's been out there two weeks. (*Silence*.) Why did you do it?

RUDYARD. Why did I do what? . . . Carrie, why did I do what?

CARRIE (*unable to resist*). Why did you push him? You could have changed his mind.

RUDYARD. I had no desire to change his . . . (*Desperately angry*.) This is not the moment.

CARRIE. I knew it would happen. He should never have gone, and you should never have bullied him.

RUDYARD. Stop this.

CARRIE. Pushing, never letting up.

RUDYARD. This is so wrong of you.

CARRIE. Could he be captured? Could he? If they find out he's your son . . . would they know he's your son? When did we send his new I.D. disk?

RUDYARD. I'm not sure.

CARRIE. It was over a week ago, over a week, he'll be wearing it, they'll know, they'll torture him.

RUDYARD. Calm down.

CARRIE. They hate you so much, they'll torture him . . .

RUDYARD. Be quiet! For one moment.

Silence.

CARRIE. I'd like a whisky.

RUDYARD. Right. (*He organises two whiskies*.)

CARRIE. I can't bear to think of him in pain.

RUDYARD. No.

Silence.

Do you really blame me for this? . . . Do you? . . . You do. . . . do you Carrie?

CARRIE. You should have stopped him.

RUDYARD. All of Jack's friends, to a man, every one of them, is in France. Do you think for one moment that I could have dissuaded him?

CARRIE. The point is, that you never tried.

RUDYARD. No I didn't.

CARRIE. Nor did you want to stop him.

RUDYARD. No . . . Why should I? Why should I stop him? If I had, he would have suffered a living death here, ashamed and despised by everyone. Could you bear that? . . . It's true. How would he hold his head up, whilst his friends risked death in France? How would he walk down the high street, or into a shop? He wouldn't. He would stay indoors, growing weaker and quieter by the day. Unable to leave his room. And he would wish he was dead.

CARRIE. People would understand.

RUDYARD. No they would not. They know what we are fighting for. They know we must go forward, willing to sacrifice everything to deliver mankind from evil.

CARRIE. Yes that's very fine. But will you believe that tomorrow? Today is the last day you can believe that.

RUDYARD. Carrie, if by any chance Jack is dead, it will have been the finest moment in his young life. We would not wish him to outlive that.

CARRIE. You don't believe that Rud. I know you don't. There is no need to say that to me.

Long pause. RUDYARD *says nothing. Then the door is flung open and* ELSIE *is there. She is carrying four unwrapped birthday presents, plus brown paper, string, labels, scissors, etc. She dumps it all on the table.*

ELSIE Hello!

RUDYARD. Hello Bird.

ELSIE. What are you drinking?

RUDYARD. Whisky.

ELSIE. But it's only a quarter to twelve.

RUDYARD. Well never mind. It tastes jolly good.

ELSIE *holds up a paper bag with something in it.*

ELSIE. This is from Jack. I think he'd approve.

She looks at CARRIE, *then* RUDYARD. *Silence.*

He's been killed.

RUDYARD. No . . . no he's missing.

ELSIE. Missing?

RUDYARD. Believed wounded.

ELSIE says nothing. Silence. She looks at her parents. She then picks up a piece of wrapping paper and folds it in two, creasing it sharply. She cuts down the crease and places a present on one of the halves of paper. She carefully wraps it. RUDYARD *and* CARRIE *watch her.*

RUDYARD. Bird . . .

ELSIE. He'll come home then . . . he'll be fine. How are we doing for time?

CARRIE. Not well.

ELSIE. Mother?

She hands a present and a sheet of paper to CARRIE. ELSIE *picks up some string and neatly ties up her parcel.*

Mother?

CARRIE *starts to wrap her parcel.* RUDYARD *picks up a piece of paper.*

RUDYARD. Do we need to go?

ELSIE. Very rude if we don't. At this notice.

RUDYARD *wraps his parcel. No-one says anything. The sounds of paper, scissors, wooden boxes on a table.* ELSIE *cuts lengths of string and then writes her label. She passes pen and label to* CARRIE. CARRIE *writes her label.* ELSIE *takes* JOHN*'s present out of the bag. Suddenly she is still. She looks at* RUDYARD.

Why did you let him go?

RUDYARD *struggles to control his anger.*

RUDYARD. No sacrifice . . . is too great . . . no sacrifice, however painful, is too great . . . if we win the day . . .

ELSIE (*angry and upset*). You've missed the point haven't you? God! You just . . . You've no idea. God!

Silence. RUDYARD *and* CARRIE *are helpless.*

Don't you realise, he didn't give a damn about your cause? The reason he went to France, the reason he went to get his head shot off, was to get away from us! He couldn't bear us any more.

Short silence.

The suffocation, the love, the expectation. That's why he went. To escape this dark, depressing house. To be rid of us, to be rid of home. (RUDYARD *and* CARRIE *say nothing*.)

What does that do to your theories Father? Is that reason enough to fight? Is that an honourable sacrifice? A fair exchange? Is it? (*She starts to cry*.) Is it? Is it? I don't think so.

ELSIE *cries her eyes out*. RUDYARD *and* CARRIE *are utterly speechless. No-one moves. Lights down slowly*.

End of Scene One.

ACT TWO SCENE TWO

1904. A memory. Batemans.

Pitch black. RUDYARD, JOHN, *and* ELSIE *lie under a tarpaulin on the drawing room floor.* JOHN *is seven years old,* ELSIE *is nine. The window is open. Outside, heavy summer rain pours down.* RUDYARD's *voice is heard in the dark.*

RUDYARD. Ready?

A moment, then RUDYARD *switches on a torch and a beam of light hits the ceiling.*

I'm the Pole Star. Jack, I want you to find . . . Cassiopeia.

JOHN. Cassiopeia?

RUDYARD. Cassiopeia. Torch on.

JOHN *switches on his torch. A second beam hits the ceiling.*

Off you go.

The beam of JOHN's *torch circles 'the sky' a couple of times before settling on a spot.*

That's not bad at all. A little to your left. No! Other way. Left! A little more . . . whoah. Up a fraction. That's it. I reckon that's pretty good. And what letter of the alphabet does Cassiopeia resemble?

JOHN. 'W'.

RUDYARD. Absolutely right. Mind you she may look like a 'W' but actually she's the queen of Ethiopia . . . Join me in the middle.

JOHN *merges the beam of his torch with* RUDYARD*'s*.

Bird are you playing?

ELSIE. I wanted to sleep outdoors.

RUDYARD. So did I, but we can do that any old time. Camping indoors is something special. Are you playing?

ELSIE *puts out her hand.* RUDYARD *hands her* JOHN*'s torch.*

What about . . . Ursa Major?

ELSIE*'s torch beam crashes to somewhere near the North Pole.*

No! You're trillions of miles out. Try again. (*She does so.*) That's better. That's much better. Up a little bit. Too much. Back. That's it. Ursa Major. Otherwise known as . . . ?

JOHN. The Great Bear.

RUDYARD. Or?

ELSIE. The Plough.

RUDYARD. Very good. Join me in the middle.

ELSIE*'s beam merges with* RUDYARD*'s.*

The Pole Star – the brightest of 'em all. Admiral Jack Kipling's star. Alone at night, on the bridge of his ship, The Pole Star is his closest companion.

They turn off their torches. RUDYARD *switches on a lamp. The children settle, until only their heads are visible.*

JOHN. I want to be an astronomer.

RUDYARD. Good idea . . . now we have a choice. A tale of the Admiral, slicing through the icy Baltic? Or a tale of the Grand Trunk Road?

JOHN. The Grand Trunk Road.

RUDYARD. Right you are.

JOHN. With Captain Jack Kipling.

RUDYARD. Captain Kipling of the Bengal Lancers, finest cavalry officer of his generation – straight-backed, tight-kneed, keen-eyed, he patrols the Grand Trunk Road. Have you heard about that great road?

JOHN. Tell me again.

RUDYARD. It is the longest road in India. The backbone of all
    Hindustan. 1500 miles and straight as a ruler. All castes and
    kinds of men move here. It is a river of life as nowhere else
    exists in the world. Look Jack! Here comes a gang of long-
    haired Sansis, carrying baskets of lizards. Don't approach
    them, they are deep pollution. And there's an Akali, a wild-
    eyed, wild-haired Sikh. Look at the boys prancing on stilts
    made of sugar cane, look at the big-bosomed earth carriers . . .
    There's a juggler, and a dancing bear, and a seller of sacred
    Ganges water . . . all the world going and coming. But all the
    world stops to watch Captain Jack Kipling trot by. But what's
    the commotion? There's a fight, there's a cart overturned, Jack
    Kipling canters over in a cloud of dust and leaps from his
    pony. A tall, grey-bearded man is stealing fruit from an
    innocent woman, and a Punjabi police constable looks on,
    doing nothing. The man sees Jack Kipling arrive, and with a
    tiny silver dagger, stabs at his thigh . . . you're hurt, but not
    badly, a crimson stain appears on your white breeches, you're
    angry, the injustice of it, an innocent fruit seller! You draw
    your sabre, and bring the flat of the blade crashing down on the
    tall man's head. Not dead, but very nearly. The fruit seller is
    overjoyed and gives you fresh mangos for your journey, and
    binds your wounded thigh with a strip of blue, Indian silk. You
    admonish the police constable for indifference and ride on your
    way. Captain Jack Kipling of the Bengal Lancers patrolling the
    Grand Trunk Road. What do you think Jack? Do you think that
    would suit? Jack? Are you asleep?

He is.

ELSIE (*nine years*). And what will I be?

RUDYARD. You will meet and marry Captain Jack Kipling's
    oldest friend. A Lieutenant in the Hussars. And by coincidence,
    it transpires that he hails from Sussex. He has an estate on the
    edge of the Ashdown Forest. So, you will settle with your
    Lieutenant, who was decorated for bravery and slightly
    wounded in the Afghan Wars, you will settle in a rambling
    rectory near Lamberhurst, only a mile or two from your
    Mother and Father. You will have five children, two boys and
    three girls, and you shall all visit us here at Batemans. And we
    will sit in the garden and compare notes over a cup of tea. How
    does that sound?

ELSIE. I like it.

RUDYARD. Good.

Silence.

Anyone awake?

ELSIE. No.

RUDYARD. Good.

> RUDYARD *switches off the lamp.*

> *End of Scene Two.*

ACT TWO SCENE THREE

September 1917.

Two years later. John is still missing. RUDYARD *sits at his desk exhausted.*

The guns of Passchendale can be heard in the background.

RUDYARD. Tired, tired to the tiredest degree.

> RUDYARD *closes his eyes.* CARRIE *enters excited.*

CARRIE. That was encouraging wasn't it? Captain Bruce's story tallies perfectly. A genuine lead. Isn't it exciting? Rud . . . ?

RUDYARD. Sorry.

> CARRIE *goes to the bookcase – one shelf is full of identically bound files.*

CARRIE. I need last summer's interviews (*She pulls out two files.*) July, August . . . was it Lieutenant Grayson or Cuthbert? Cuthbert I think . . . he said exactly the same thing. Can you remember?

RUDYARD. Sorry, what?

CARRIE. Grayson or Cuthbert?

RUDYARD. I'm not with you.

CARRIE. Yes you are. Oh, come on, this is so exciting. (*Going to the table.*) Could I have Bruce's notes? (RUDYARD *gives them to her.*) Thank you.

> CARRIE *dumps the files on the floor and spreads out Bruce's notes beside them. She finds the relevant section.*

CARRIE. Here we are. Listen to this, it ties in perfectly . . . Bruce says: 'I am practically certain that I saw Lieutenant Kipling leading his platoon around the southern tip of Chalk Pit Wood in the direction of the colliery head at Puits Bis 14 . . . ' That's exactly what Cuthbert said. Was it Cuthbert? It was wasn't it?

RUDYARD. It may well have been.

CARRIE *unties the July file and spreads out the interview sheets on the floor. She picks up one sheet, the index, and reads down the list.*

CARRIE. Callum, Carstairs, Chater, Clifford, Deighton . . . Oh. Perhaps it was August. When was the heatwave? It was boiling hot, we interviewed him in the garden. Do you remember?

RUDYARD. I don't off hand, no.

CARRIE. You're not trying very hard.

CARRIE *unwraps the August file. More papers on the floor. She reads the August index.*

Carghill, Carter, Chester, Crichton, Critchley, Dreyfuss. No. Was it Grayson then?

RUDYARD. I really don't remember Carrie.

CARRIE. I can't believe you're just sitting there.

CARRIE *looks through the August index.*

Gibbons and Grantly. No Grayson. I'm sure it was July. Where did I put the July index? I had it seconds ago, where's the other index? Did you see where I put it?

RUDYARD. It must be there somewhere.

CARRIE. You're just sitting there . . . ah.

CARRIE *finds the index.*

. . . no 'G's at all.

(*Returning to the bookcase.*) Perhaps it was June. It could have been that early actually.

ELSIE *enters.*

Bird, we've made a breakthrough.

ELSIE. Have we?

CARRIE. Yes, oh yes.

ELSIE. That's wonderful.

CARRIE. I'm trying to remember who it was we interviewed last summer, I thought it was Cuthbert or Grayson, but anyway, they said they'd spotted Jack on the northern, no, southern tip . . . Bird would you give me a hand, Rud is being singularly unhelpful.

ELSIE. Should we do it later?

CARRIE. No let's do it now.

ELSIE. I don't think we can.

CARRIE. Why not?

ELSIE. There's one more interview.

CARRIE. It can wait.

ELSIE. He's here now.

CARRIE. Who is he?

ELSIE. Mr. Frankland.

CARRIE. Mr?

ELSIE. He's not an Irish Guard. He's not a soldier.

CARRIE. Then why's he coming?

ELSIE. I don't know, he insisted on seeing Father.

CARRIE. Well, bring him in, I'll speak to him. I'm sure he'll understand if we ask him to come back another time.

ELSIE *exits.* RUDYARD *gets up suddenly from his chair.*

RUDYARD. He will not understand, nor do I want him to understand. We'll check the files tonight.

CARRIE. No, we should do it now, while Captain Bruce's interview is fresh in the mind.

RUDYARD. No. Sorry. No.

CARRIE *is sorting through the interview sheets. They are now hopelessly muddled up.*

CARRIE. Oh, God. They're all mixed up now . . . July, July, August, July . . . for goodness sake Rud please, give me a hand.

RUDYARD. I didn't get them out.

CARRIE. No, you haven't done anything.

RUDYARD. No that's right. You're right, you're right, you're absolutely right, I am unutterably selfish. I've interviewed 350 Irish Guards over the last two years, I've postponed my literary career in order to write a history of the Guards for our son, for no remuneration, which don't misunderstand me, I have enjoyed doing, I wanted to do it, and I shall continue to do it. But of course you're right, I am as lazy as sin, I am the most self-centred, useless, insensitive man . . .

CARRIE. Oh, don't do that.

RUDYARD. Do what?

CARRIE. It's a performance.

RUDYARD. It is not a performance. I'm agreeing with you, I should be chastised.

CARRIE. All I'm asking is, that you help me identify the person who saw Jack alive in the same place and the same time as Captain Bruce. It's a positive link, it's a ray of hope, isn't it? Isn't it?

RUDYARD. It may be.

CARRIE. Please.

RUDYARD (*exasperated*). Oh, give me some.

CARRIE. Not if that's your reaction.

RUDYARD. Give me some, I'll do some.

CARRIE *hands* RUDYARD *a pile of papers*.

What am I looking for?

CARRIE. Check the 'C's and 'G's for an interview by someone with a name similar to Cuthbert or Grayson.

RUDYARD. This is the wrong moment.

CARRIE. It won't take long.

RUDYARD. It will take hours.

CARRIE. We can make a start.

RUDYARD. It's the wrong moment Carrie. Mr. Frankland is here. I'm not doing it. I'm sorry, I'm too tired.

CARRIE. Alright, I'll do it myself.

RUDYARD (*exploding with fury*). No, we are not doing it *now!*

He grabs CARRIE*'s pile of papers, and flings them across the room. Papers fly all over the place.*

I am not trawling through these bloody files to support a tenuous link between Captain Bruce and Lieutenant 'whoever he is' who may or may not have seen something similar over a year ago. I'm not, it's pointless.

CARRIE. You've given up hope.

RUDYARD. No, no I haven't. I haven't at all. Carrie I understand. I understand your desire to discover the truth, but two brief sightings, early in the battle, do not constitute proof that he is alive.

CARRIE. It's a start.

RUDYARD. He's been missing for two years.

CARRIE *sits on the floor, and starts to collect the papers together.*

I'd like a cigarette.

CARRIE. That won't help.

RUDYARD. Have you hidden them?

CARRIE. I threw them away.

RUDYARD. Oh.

Silence.

(*An idea.*) I know.

RUDYARD *walks to the bookcase and pulls out the same book that John pulled out four years earlier. Behind it* RUDYARD *discovers a crumpled old packet of half-finished cigarettes.*

Not mine, Jack's.

They are silent. They stare at the cigarettes.

I found them years ago. He should have chosen another author. I'm always dipping into Trollope.

RUDYARD *replaces the book. He takes out a cigarette.*

I wonder how four years will affect the taste.

CARRIE. May I see?

RUDYARD *passes her the packet. He then collects an ashtray and joins* CARRIE *on the floor. They sit in a sea of white paper.* CARRIE *stares at the cigarettes.* RUDYARD *lights up.*

(*Very moved.*) How strange. Why should this be so sad?

RUDYARD (*taking a drag and coughing horribly*). Allah be praised!

CARRIE. That is precisely why you shouldn't smoke.

RUDYARD (*coughing again*). Fouler than foul.

He stubs it out. They sit in silence for a moment.

CARRIE. It's not your brand.

RUDYARD. No. A gesture of defiance.

Silence.

CARRIE (*quietly*). We'll find you Jack.

RUDYARD. We will.

ELSIE *enters with* MR. FRANKLAND. *She looks down at her parents who, for a moment, remain sitting on the floor.*

ELSIE. This is Mr. Frankland.

RUDYARD. Ah.

ELSIE. What happened?

CARRIE *ignores* ELSIE*'s question, and gets up to greet* FRANKLAND.

CARRIE. Good afternoon Mr. Frankland. I'm Carrie Kipling.

FRANKLAND. Pleased to meet you.

CARRIE. This is my husband, Rudyard Kipling.

FRANKLAND. Pleased to meet you. I recognise you from pictures of course . . .

RUDYARD. I'm sorry about the chaos.

FRANKLAND. Oh, that's alright . . .

RUDYARD. As you can see a file exploded without warning.

FRANKLAND. Oh dear . . . I can easily come back.

ELSIE. No, no, of course not.

CARRIE (*overlapping*). Well perhaps . . .

FRANKLAND. If it's a bad moment . . .

ELSIE. No, no, it's not.

Silence. ELSIE *looks to* RUDYARD *to take over, but he is silent and looks exhausted.*

ELSIE. I didn't introduce myself, I'm Elsie.

FRANKLAND. I thought so. You must be Una?

ELSIE. Una?

FRANKLAND. In 'Puck of Pook's Hill'? Sorry, I . . .

ELSIE. Oh, yes I am! I absolutely am. I didn't . . . quite . . .

FRANKLAND. No, doesn't matter. No.

Silence.

RUDYARD. Right . . . this mess.

FRANKLAND. Would you like some help?

RUDYARD. No thank you . . .

Silence. ELSIE covers.

ELSIE. Did you like 'Puck of Pook's Hill'?

FRANKLAND. Oh, it's my favourite book, I think, really.

ELSIE. Is it?

FRANKLAND. Oh, yes. We used to go hop picking, when I was a kid, in the summer . . . it reminded me, you know, I mean the descriptions of the countryside an' that . . . and I loved all the history bits, so . . . I think it's brilliant . . . look, it is a bad moment, if I could make another appointment, and come back some other time.

ELSIE. No. Definitely not. Now is fine, isn't it Father?

RUDYARD. Of course.

CARRIE. How do you feel you can help us? . . . You're not in the Irish Guards are you?

FRANKLAND. Well, I'm not in anything now, with my leg . . . but, before, I was a rifleman – King's Own Rifle Corps.

CARRIE. Because my husband's book is a history of the Irish Guards, my son's regiment you see.

FRANKLAND. That's right, I knew that, yes.

CARRIE. Mr. Kipling's really only interviewing officers and soldiers from the Irish Guards.

FRANKLAND. Yes, I understand that.

ELSIE. Oh. Then . . .

FRANKLAND. But I read in the papers you were also looking for information about your son . . . John.

Long silence.

ELSIE. Yes.

RUDYARD. We are, yes.

CARRIE. Do you know something?

FRANKLAND. Well, I don't, no. But I brought someone with me. . . I hope that's not presumptuous.

RUDYARD. No.

FRANKLAND. He's very keen to talk to you.

RUDYARD. Who is he?

FRANKLAND. An Irish Guard. I've left him in the hall, I sort of, don't want to leave him alone for too long, he gets very, you know, he was very nervous about coming.

RUDYARD. How do you know him?

FRANKLAND. Next door beds in hospital, in Surrey. I lent him one of your books, 'Kim' as it happens, which I love, the bit on the road in India, love it, he liked it too actually, and we got talking, and it turned out he knew your son John.

RUDYARD. I see.

FRANKLAND. We could come back at a better time . . .

CARRIE. No, we'd like to talk to him now.

FRANKLAND. Sure that's alright?

RUDYARD. Absolutely.

FRANKLAND. Shall I fetch him in then?

RUDYARD. I think so, yes.

FRANKLAND. Right.

CARRIE. Does he know what happened to John?

FRANKLAND. Well . . . I think I'll leave him to . . . you know, it's better really.

CARRIE. Can you, just, tell us if he's alive?

FRANKLAND. Do you mind if I leave it to him . . . I do think it'd be better . . . shall I?

RUDYARD. Yes please.

FRANKLAND *leaves to fetch the soldier.* RUDYARD, CARRIE, *and* ELSIE *are silent. Then.*

CARRIE. Rud . . .

RUDYARD. Let's wait and see.

CARRIE. He wouldn't come if he didn't know something.

RUDYARD. Come on, let's clear these up.

They pick up papers. Long silence.

ELSIE. They should be back by now.

RUDYARD. Give them a moment.

They continue to pick up papers.

ELSIE. What are they doing? Perhaps they lost their nerve, perhaps they've gone.

RUDYARD. No, no.

Another silence. Then FRANKLAND *and* BOWE *are at the door.* BOWE *is clearly very distressed. He is gasping for breath.*

BOWE. Thank God for the light.

He lifts his head and sucks in air.

FRANKLAND. I shouldn't have left him alone.

BOWE. Jesus, I can't breathe. I can't breathe.

FRANKLAND. Deep breaths.

BOWE. I can't get the air in.

FRANKLAND (*to* RUDYARD *and* ELSIE). Could you open the window.

BOWE. It's the gas.

FRANKLAND (*urgently*). The window.

ELSIE *opens the windows.*

BOWE (*struggling*). I need my mask, let go o' me, I need my mask.

FRANKLAND. You're alright Michael. We'll get you some fresh air.

BOWE. It's our own gas, we're after walkin' through our own gas.

FRANKLAND. Come on. You're safe here.

BOWE. The bastards have got the range wrong.

FRANKLAND. It's my fault.

BOWE (*terrified*). Look at it.

FRANKLAND. I should never have left him alone.

BOWE. It's like a live creature.

He is seeing the chlorine gas, heavier than air, moving along, just above the ground.

FRANKLAND. There's nothing there. Breathe deeply.

BOWE. Help me.

FRANKLAND. You're alright, breathe deeply.

BOWE. Help me.

FRANKLAND *holds* BOWE *facing the window. He breathes the fresh air.*

FRANKLAND. Keep breathing.

ELSIE. Would you like a drink?

BOWE *is leaning out of the window, lapping up the air.*

Would he like a drink of something?

FRANKLAND. A glass of water.

ELSIE *leaves to fetch water.* BOWE *slumps to the floor, shaking uncontrollably.*

BOWE. Thomas Jolly, Jimmy . . . Jimmy . . . Thomas Jolly, Jimmy . . . Jimmy McLelland, Thomas Jolly, Jimmy McLelland, Paddy, yes, Thomas Jolly, Jimmy McLelland, Paddy McMahon, Docherty, Corporal Docherty, Guardsman, Guardsman, Guardsman George McHugh, O'Leary, me, and the Lieutenant . . .

FRANKLAND. Michael . . .

BOWE. Is that it? There should be eight. Was that eight? Thomas Jolly, Jimmy Mcmahon, no, Jimmy McLelland, Jimmy McLelland, Paddy McMahon and . . . Paddy McMahon and . . . and . . . Jesus I can't remember, I had it a moment ago, why can't I remember? I can't remember the simplest things, Jesus you'd think it was easy enough. There should always be eight . . . Oh, God stop me shakin', stop me shakin' . . .

RUDYARD. Shall I close the window?

BOWE. No, don't close the window . . . don't close the window, please, please . . .

FRANKLAND. We won't.

ELSIE *returns with a glass of water.*

Michael . . . water. Here, Michael, water.

FRANKLAND *holds the glass to* BOWE's *lips. Most of it spills, but some of it goes down. It seems to calm him a little.*

BOWE. Eight of us, eight of us made it to the woods.

RUDYARD. What was the name of the wood?

BOWE (*very methodically*). Thomas Jolly . . . Jimmy McLelland . . . Paddy McMahon . . . Corporal Docherty . . . George McHugh . . . Sergeant O'Leary . . . the Lieutenant.

FRANKLAND. What was the Lieutenant's name?

BOWE. Eight made it to the woods, it was a great triumph . . . a great success. I wasn't scared, not at all.

FRANKLAND. Michael, what was the name of your Lieutenant?

A louder explosion, heard through the open window, attracts BOWE's *attention.*

BOWE. . . . D'yous hear that, they're after killin' each other as we speak . . . can y' hear 'em? Where's it coming from?

RUDYARD. Passchendaele.

BOWE. Passchendaele? Never heard of it . . . How far is it from here?

RUDYARD. A hundred miles?

BOWE. Jesus.

FRANKLAND. Michael . . . this is Rudyard Kipling.

BOWE (*to* RUDYARD). I'm so sorry, I hate the dark, I'm sorry to make such a fuss, thass a pitch black room you've got there, I hate the dark . . . (*Pause.*) The soldiers are after singin' your verses at the front, did yous know that?

RUDYARD. It's very flattering.

Short silence.

I believe you knew my son?

BOWE. D'yous mind if I smoke?

RUDYARD. Go ahead.

BOWE (*his hand trembles as he tries to get a cigarette out. He drops the packet*). Useless.

RUDYARD. Let me. (*He picks up the packet.*)

BOWE. Useless.

RUDYARD. I shall enjoy lighting it for you.

BOWE. Have one.

RUDYARD. I'm not allowed.

BOWE. I never smoked myself, before we went to France, I've a farm in County Clare, an' at home it never crossed my mind, now I can't stop.

RUDYARD *takes one luxuriant drag and hands the cigarette to* BOWE. *They watch silently as* BOWE *takes a couple of deep drags. His trembling stops, and he appears to fall asleep. He drops the cigarette.* FRANKLAND *picks it up, still burning.*

FRANKLAND. Come on.

FRANKLAND *picks* BOWE *up.* RUDYARD *helps. They lead him to the sofa. He sits and stares vaguely ahead of him. Then.*

BOWE (*to* FRANKLAND). You're after droppin' ash on the beautiful carpet.

FRANKLAND. Am I? I'm sorry.

BOWE (*to* RUDYARD). Where's it from?

RUDYARD. What?

BOWE. The carpet.

RUDYARD. Persia.

BOWE. Oh, is it a Persian carpet? Beautiful colours. Aren't they beautiful colours? Persian, I've always wondered . . . it's a beautiful carpet.

Silence.

RUDYARD. You knew my son.

BOWE. Always worried about my feet.

ELSIE. Your feet?

BOWE. Examined them three times a week. Powdered them the day we went over, they were in a dreadful state, on account o' the rain.

CARRIE. Was it raining? Was it raining? On the day . . .

BOWE. The Lieutenant said we brought the rain with us from Ireland.

CARRIE. When? When was this? . . . John . . . on the day you . . . with Jack, what date was this, can you remember?

RUDYARD. Just a moment Carrie . . .

CARRIE. Was it raining when you attacked the wood?

RUDYARD. Carrie, please . . . You knew my son?

FRANKLAND. What was your platoon Michael?

BOWE. '3' Platoon. Guardsman Michael Bowe 7786, '3' Platoon, 'B' Company, 2nd Battalion, Irish Guards.

RUDYARD. Then my son, Lieutenant John Kipling was your Platoon Commander.

BOWE. Very gentle. Very kind.

RUDYARD. He was your Platoon Commander.

BOWE. The Lieutenant was good to me.

RUDYARD. When were you wounded?

BOWE. Me and McHugh lay in a shell hole all day. An' Jimmy was there, but he died, an' we watched the rats and the flies move in on him. Slowly at first, like they weren't quite sure . . . three steps forward and two steps back you know, like they expected him to open his eyes and sit up. But they got more confident as the day went on.

RUDYARD. Was this the Battle of Loos?

BOWE. Chalk Pit Wood.

RUDYARD. Yes. Battle of Loos.

BOWE. Lyin', watchin' our blood soak into the chalk.

RUDYARD. Would you tell me about that day Mr. Bowe, the attack on Chalk Pit Wood?

BOWE (*nervously*). I didn't want to come here. I didn't want to come, I don't want to talk about it really . . .

RUDYARD. But you did come.

BOWE. . . . To explain something . . . I wanted to . . . explain something . . . but I can't . . . I think I'd like to go home . . . can I go home? Would yous mind? . . . I'm so tired.

BOWE *stands up and tries to leave.* FRANKLAND *grabs his arm.*

FRANKLAND. You wanted to tell them.

BOWE. I'm tired.

FRANKLAND. You said you'd tell them.

BOWE. I should've stayed. I should've helped. I shouldn't've run . . . I should've helped.

RUDYARD. Helped who?

BOWE. I'm so tired.

RUDYARD. Who should you have helped?

FRANKLAND. Michael . . . sit down. Sit down Michael.

BOWE *(as he sits)*. I'd like to go home.

RUDYARD. You wanted to explain something . . . Mr. Bowe . . . what was it you wanted to tell us? . . . Please. Did Lieutenant Kipling lead you over the top? Did he blow the whistle?

BOWE. He was my Platoon Commander.

RUDYARD. Yes.

BOWE. So he blew the whistle.

RUDYARD. Mr. Bowe, I've been interviewing Irish Guards every day for over a year. You are the first soldier I've met, from my son's Platoon, who took part in the attack on Chalk Pit Wood. Like you, we are awful tired. If you know something, anything, that will help us, we would be very grateful. To know concretely one way or the other . . . after two years . . . would be a great release for the whole family.

Silence.

ELSIE. Please.

Silence.

BOWE. The waitin' to go over's the worst . . . You want to talk to your man next to yous, but you can't. The skin on your face is stretched so tight, you feel if you speak, it'd split and peel away. . . you're on your own . . . completely. . . d'you know what I see when I do go over the top?

RUDYARD. What?

BOWE. A game of football! A bunch of arseholes dribblin' a
football across no man's land . . . the next regiment's attackin'
the Boche – with their rifles shouldered, kickin' a football . . .
in mid-air the ball disappears, and they start fallin' over – all of
'em . . . there's a bloke stridin' out with a walkin' stick, like a
gent on a Sunday jaunt in Phoenix Park. He disappears into the
smoke . . . then the machine guns . . . the Maxims . . . I dump
the shovel, I've got no choice. The bullets are all around me –
Bees! Bees! – a swarm of angry bees. Buzzin' an' racin' past
the ear. Jimmy Doyle shoutin' at me: 'We're the only two left
Michael.' . . . he's hit! He goes down . . . I'm runnin' and my
lungs are burstin'. The din is diabolic, so loud you can't hear
it, you can only feel it, feel the whole planet tremblin'. But
I make it . . . I fall into Jerry's front line trench . . . I'm lyin' on
top o' somethin', lyin' there tryin' to breathe, lyin' on top of a
dead man . . . practically kissin' him I'm so close to him. My
uniform is soakin' wet, I look down an' the front of him is
gone, an' all his insides are spillin' over the edge of him . . .
covered in his blood, German blood. Then . . . Jesus . . . I see
the gas creepin' towards me, like somethin' livin' an' I know
I've lost my mask. Help me Jesus, where's me fuckin' mask?
. . . the gas is round me, creepin' up me. Where's me fuckin'
mask! Where's me mask! I'm breathin' it, I'm goin' to die, I'm
dyin'. But the German's mask is in his hand, Mother o' God
thank you, I pull it away from him, holdin' it against my face,
breathin' the clean air, Jesus, I'm goin'to live. An' this Hun is
after savin' my life . . . someone is beside me, givin' me the
thumbs up in front of my face. I stick my thumb in the air, he's
pointin' down the trench. There's more lads down there and
an officer . . . makin' our way down the trench . . . there's a
body . . . Jesus this is what it's like, there's a body standin'
there, standin' casual like, but he's got no head . . . this is what
it's like . . . water . . . Jesus, my lips . . . water . . .

FRANKLAND (*to* ELSIE). More water?

ELSIE. Right.

BOWE. A drink.

> BOWE *leans his head on a cushion and rests. His mouth is
> dry. He licks his lips.*

Water . . .

ELSIE. Would you like a drink Mr. Frankland?

FRANKLAND. That's very kind, no thank you.

ELSIE. Are you sure?

FRANKLAND. Quite sure, thank you.

> ELSIE *leaves. The room is quiet.* BOWE *now lies on the sofa, his eyes half closed.* RUDYARD *pours two whiskies. He hands one to* CARRIE, *who takes it without saying anything. He walks to the window and looks out. A moment of stillness. Then he returns to his table and picks up a packet of cigarettes. He lights one for himself and one for* BOWE. *He perches on the sofa by* BOWE's *head and hands him a cigarette.*

RUDYARD. Mr. Bowe . . .

> BOWE *takes the cigarette.*

BOWE. . . . A drink o' water . . .

RUDYARD. It's on it's way . . . tired?

BOWE. Yes.

RUDYARD. Would you like to go upstairs and rest?

BOWE. I'm alright here . . . (*Re.* RUDYARD's *cigarette.*) I thought yous weren't allowed?

RUDYARD. I'm not. That's why it tastes so good.

> *Silence.*

You're a farmer?

BOWE. Yes.

RUDYARD. In County Clare?

BOWE. Yes.

RUDYARD. It's a beautiful part of Ireland.

BOWE. I miss it. I miss the animals.

RUDYARD. I'm sure.

BOWE. Every time I get better they're after sending me back to France. An' as soon as I'm near the front . . . I get the shakes again . . . an' I'm good for nothin'. D'you think they'll give up on me? Maybe they'll send me home . . . could yous stub it out for me? My mouth's too dry . . .

> RUDYARD *puts out* BOWE's *cigarette.* ELSIE *returns with water for* BOWE.

FRANKLAND. Thank you.

RUDYARD. Here we are.

RUDYARD *helps* BOWE *drink the water.*

When you advanced, when you crossed no-man's land . . .

BOWE. I wasn't scared at all you know, not at all, don't yous think that's strange? I was before, and after I was, but not during, no thoughts o' gettin' killed, nothin' . . . I think the winter conditions in Clare were a help to me, wadin' through the mud on the farm you know . . .

RUDYARD. Were you at all, during the attack itself, in any way . . . uplifted, or excited . . .

BOWE. Not excited, not scared, nothin' . . . Too much else to think about to be anythin'.

RUDYARD. You got to the German trenches, and some guardsmen and an officer were already there?

BOWE. Eight of us made it . . .

RUDYARD. The officer was Lieutenant Kipling?

BOWE. Yes.

RUDYARD. How did he seem?

BOWE. What do you mean?

RUDYARD. Well, was he calm or . . . excited or . . . nervous . . . ?

BOWE. He was fine, you know, jus' fine.

RUDYARD. Did he seem . . . pleased to be there?

BOWE. Pleased? No-one's pleased to be there. He was fine. He told us we had to go on.

RUDYARD. Did he?

BOWE. 'We've only just arrived,' says George McHugh, 'We have to go on,' says the Lieutenant.

RUDYARD. Was he anxious? Was he worried about continuing?

BOWE. No, he was very firm about it. We're to advance through Chalk Pit Wood, an' take the second line o' trenches.

RUDYARD. And you did?

BOWE. The wood was on fire, we couldn't go through, we'd be burned alive. But suddenly the rain comes down, like a blanket, like God puttin' out the flames, an'we trot through the wood, free as birds, no shootin', no shellin', nothin', into the trenches on the other side.

Silence.

But then we see it. Ahead of us. An' we know they've jus' been waitin' for us.

RUDYARD. What did you see?

BOWE. 'Puits Bis 14.'

ELSIE. What's that?

BOWE. Made of black iron, lookin' down on us, like it was alive, 50, 100ft, high. 'Puits Bis 14.' An' all the way up it, there's platforms, an' on every platform there's a machine gun. The Lieutenant tells us that's what we're here for, he tells us we're to attack the machine gun post on 'Puits Bis 14.' George McHugh is after screamin' at him that we'll all be killed, an' the Lieutenant tells us we've no choice. 'You're a fuckin' murderer,' screams George, 'We've got no choice,' says the Lieutenant . . . there's only eight of us, only eight of us, they're waitin', watchin' an' waitin' . . . an' I start to shake, there's nothin' I can do, I can't breathe, I can't get the air in, it's not my fault, I can't help it, an' he blows the whistle again, we're goin' again, I pull myself over the edge, but my body won't work, I can't stand up, I'm tryin' so hard, but I can't . . . an' I don't know how, I can't remember how, but I'm lyin' in the bottom of a hole, lyin in water, an' there's a body floatin' beside me, I'm lyin in the water, lookin' up . . . lookin' up . . .

BOWE *is very upset.*

RUDYARD. Yes?

BOWE. I look up . . .

RUDYARD. Yes.

BOWE. An' I see . . . I see . . . I can't . . . I see . . .

RUDYARD. What?

BOWE. I see Lieutenant Kipling. He's . . . standin' . . . on the edge . . . the bottom of his face is . . .

RUDYARD. Go on.

BOWE. I . . .

RUDYARD *grabs* BOWE*'s hand.*

RUDYARD. Go on please.

BOWE. The bottom of his face is . . . shot away.

CARRIE. Jack.

BOWE. There's nothin' below his top lip, nothin' at all. He's cryin', tears, cryin' with the pain sir.

CARRIE. Jack.

BOWE. Then George McHugh's in the hole with me. He's screamin', 'Run, for fuck's sake, run, we've got to get back, dump your kit, we're runnin', we're fuckin' runnin',' 'No, stop. It's the Lieutenant, he's hurt.' 'I don't give a fuck,' he screams. 'He's hurt, we've got to take him with us.' 'I'm not takin' anyone anywhere.' So I say: 'You go then, I'm helpin' him back.' I wanted to get him home you know, I wanted to get him home. Then McHugh grabs me by the throat: 'You soft, fuckin', bastard, yous can do what you like, but if you blather to anyone, I'll kill you, I'll shoot you through the head.' An' Jesus, he would . . . then he's gone. (*Pause.*) It's jus' me. An' the Lieutenant's cryin' with the pain . . .

RUDYARD. Did you . . . what did you do?

BOWE. That's what I wanted to explain . . .

RUDYARD. Yes.

BOWE. I wanted to say, I wanted to help him, you do believe me don't yous? You must believe me, I wanted to, you do believe me?

RUDYARD. Go on.

BOWE. He was in awful pain you see, you see, so . . . so . . .

RUDYARD. What?

BOWE. I decided . . . I made a decision sir, he was in such pain, he didn't know it was me, I don't think anything . . . would've . . .

RUDYARD. What did you do?

BOWE. I decided . . .

Silence.

I didn't want to humiliate him, an officer, by approachin' him while he was cryin'. It wouldn't have been dignified for him.

RUDYARD (*hardly able to speak*). So you didn't help him?

BOWE. No sir.

RUDYARD. You ran away.

BOWE. You understand don't yous? He wouldn't've wanted me to . . . to see him . . . like that . . . would he? He wouldn't've wanted me to know, would he?

RUDYARD. You ran.

BOWE. I went after George, and I say to myself, the first thing I do if I get back alive is report that the Lieutenant is wounded. But I've only gone a few yards, an' there's an explosion behind me an' hot air hits my back, I'm thrown on the floor. When I look back, smoke an' earth are plumin' into the sky . . . where the Lieutenant had been standin' . . . there's no sign of him. I'm sorry sir.

RUDYARD (*quietly*). Thank you . . . so . . . he was killed by a shell . . . during an attack on 'Puits Bis 14'. He led his men from the front, and was courageous in the face of considerable enemy fire.

BOWE. He was. Yes sir. Very courageous.

RUDYARD. Thank you.

BOWE. I should've helped him. I should've stayed. Forgive me.

RUDYARD. You must be hungry Mr. Bowe.

BOWE. It was wrong. I'm sorry. Forgive me.

RUDYARD. Bird, find Mr. Bowe and Mr. Frankland something to eat . . .

ELSIE. Father . . .

RUDYARD. I'd just like a moment . . .

    CARRIE *is sitting numb with shock.*

BOWE. I think about it all the time sir, I'm so sorry.

RUDYARD. Bird, come straight back.

BOWE. Shall I leave you a cigarette sir?

RUDYARD. No thank you.

FRANKLAND. Michael . . .

BOWE. I wanted to tell yous the truth you know, to explain . . .

FRANKLAND. Michael . . .

BOWE. I'm so sorry.

FRANKLAND *has to lead* BOWE *from the room.* ELSIE
follows. RUDYARD *and* CARRIE *are completely still. Then
after a long silence* CARRIE *gets up and starts to walk to the
door.*

RUDYARD. Carrie please stay.

CARRIE. I can't.

RUDYARD. Please.

CARRIE. I can't talk.

RUDYARD. You don't have to. Just stay for a moment.

CARRIE *stays.*

Would you like a drink?

Carrie shakes her head, but says nothing.

Are you sure? I'm having one.

CARRIE *doesn't respond.* RUDYARD *gets himself a whisky.*

By all accounts he was very brave.

Silence.

He didn't have a long time in the trenches. But he had his heart's
desire. So few of us have the opportunity to play our part.
Properly. But he did. He worked like the devil. It's a shame
that all the effort should end in one afternoon, but he achieved
what he set out to achieve. It was a short life, but in a sense
complete. I'm happy for him, and proud of him, aren't you?

CARRIE *doesn't move. Then.*

CARRIE. May I go now?

RUDYARD. If you want to.

But CARRIE *stays.*

CARRIE. I'm so relieved that you see the death of our only son as
such a positive and uplifting event. I am sincerely relieved that
you are at ease with it all. I mean we have to look for the good
in all this and your . . . I don't know what to call it, your
contentment shall we say, is a bonus isn't it?

RUDYARD. That's unfair.

CARRIE. Is it?

RUDYARD. Yes.

CARRIE. Oh. Sorry.

RUDYARD. That's not what I mean.

CARRIE. Well, I misunderstood you.

RUDYARD. I'm not 'at ease' as you put it.

CARRIE. No. Let's not talk.

RUDYARD. You must know that? Surely? Carrie?

CARRIE *says nothing.*

I find it a great comfort that so many are in our position, don't you? It is a common agony. A common sacrifice.

CARRIE. No I don't find that comforting. I don't care how many people it's happened to. That doesn't help me at all. Not at all . . . no.

Long silence.

RUDYARD. What are you thinking?

CARRIE. Nothing . . . really . . . but let's not pretend.

RUDYARD. What?

CARRIE. Nothing.

RUDYARD. No, I didn't hear you. What did you say?

CARRIE. Nothing.

RUDYARD. What did you say?

CARRIE. Don't perform to me.

RUDYARD. What do you mean? Carrie? What do you mean?

CARRIE. I can't bear . . . to think . . . the pain, he must have been in such pain . . . how long do you think it lasted?

RUDYARD. Not long.

CARRIE. How long? Five minutes? Ten minutes? Half an hour?

RUDYARD. No, not even five minutes.

CARRIE. Don't pretend to me.

RUDYARD. I'm not. The body will have been in shock. I doubt if he felt a thing. If you talk to any number of wounded soldiers, they'll confirm that . . . the pain only sets in later. So he was lucky. It was done with, quickly.

CARRIE. No, he wasn't lucky. Don't tell me he was lucky, or brave, or happy, or I know what you think. You made it quite clear from the beginning.

RUDYARD. What? What did I make clear?

CARRIE. You said it was the finest moment of his young life, and we wouldn't want him to outlive it.

RUDYARD. When did I say that?

CARRIE. You said it on the day . . . within five minutes of hearing that Jack was missing, you told me that it would be sad if he outlived the finest moment of his life.

RUDYARD. Did I?

CARRIE. That is exactly what you said.

RUDYARD. Well . . .

CARRIE. You believe that, yes, I know . . .

RUDYARD. Only . . .

CARRIE. So, now, nothing you say surprises me. Your cruelty doesn't surprise me. You are a cold fish, a very cold fish. But that's alright, I know that now. It doesn't hurt me, but don't pretend anymore. Jack was eighteen years and six weeks old. He died in the rain, he couldn't see a thing, he was alone, in pain, you can't persuade me there is any glory in that.

RUDYARD. I believe there is.

CARRIE. No.

RUDYARD. I believe there is.

CARRIE. You see we shouldn't talk.

RUDYARD. There is a glory.

CARRIE. No.

RUDYARD. Try to understand.

CARRIE. Oh, I understand.

RUDYARD. No, not in that world-weary, hurt fashion of yours . . .

CARRIE. I understand that we are very different.

RUDYARD. I must 'believe' in order to survive at all.

CARRIE. No I can't listen to this.

CARRIE *tries to leave.* RUDYARD *blocks her exit.*

RUDYARD. We're talking.

CARRIE. Let me past.

RUDYARD. No.

CARRIE *tries to pass* RUDYARD. *He grabs her.*

CARRIE. Let go of me.

RUDYARD. No.

CARRIE. Please.

RUDYARD. Do you want me to go down on my knees and own
up? Confess my . . . complicity. Admit that it's all down to me.
That I . . . murdered my son. I will if it satisfies you.

CARRIE. Please let go of me.

RUDYARD. Is that what you'd like me to do?

CARRIE. Please.

RUDYARD. Do you think a single day passes, when I don't
consider that possibility?

CARRIE. Let – go.

RUDYARD *releases* CARRIE.

RUDYARD. Not a single day. Many times a day. I'm not
oblivious. Of course I'm not. I think about it all the time. All
the time. And what truly terrifies me, is that if I am complicit,
inadvertently or otherwise, if I am to blame – what have I sent
him on to, if anything at all. Because, really, what possible
grounds are there for assuming our lives after death are
protected, in any way whatsoever. Which is why it is so
important that every sacrifice we make has true value, and
Jack's sacrifice is doubly glorious if there's nothing on the
other side. But then I think – how dare you, how dare you, how
could you, condemn your son to oblivion. To insensate
nothingness. How could you, do that, to Jack?

Short silence.

I think I have been happiest of all, lying in bed, knowing that
my son is asleep in the next room. And I would willingly lie
down now and sleep for an eternity, if I thought it would help
bring him back.

CARRIE *is silent.*

But 'you' believe that this isn't the whole affair. You believe
that death isn't the final word, don't you? So spiritually, in
some context, on some wavelengh, Jack is still alive.

RUDYARD *waits for a response, but gets none.*

So in a sense, if one can grasp the nettle intellectually, the final physical pain of death is irrelevant, merely transitional, it doesn't actually matter if Jack's last moments were ugly or dignified because now he is free, while we are still trapped down here . . . don't you think?

CARRIE. But I miss him.

RUDYARD. So do I.

He drops his head and cries. Silence. Then CARRIE *walks to the desk and looks at the diary.*

CARRIE. Captain Vesey and Lieutenant Leyton arrive tomorrow. Do you think Mr. Bowe will stay tonight . . . I hope not. I want him to go.

Short silence.

I feel . . . more dead than alive. When Josephine died, part of me died with her. But I sewed up the wound. I recovered, to a degree. But now I feel . . . more . . . dead than alive.

Silence.

I can feel his head on my chest, his thick hair under my fingers. I can hear his laugh. I can feel his heat against me . . .

RUDYARD. We'll manage.

CARRIE. Oh yes, we'll manage, I'm sure we will.

RUDYARD. We will.

CARRIE. Yes we'll manage. I don't doubt that. I'm going to go and find Bird. . . You're alright here?

RUDYARD. Won't you stay?

CARRIE. No, I'm going to find Bird. Will you be alright?

RUDYARD. Yes thank you.

CARRIE. Poor Elsie. On her own.

RUDYARD. Bring her back here.

CARRIE nods but says nothing. She leaves. Fade on RUDYARD *alone.*

End of Scene Three.

ACT TWO SCENE FOUR

1924. Seven years later. Drawing room, Batemans.

ELSIE *stands resplendent in her wedding dress.* CARRIE *bustles around her, holding up an embroidered button. Through the window, the sound of preparations for the reception. The sun streams into the room.*

ELSIE. No-one will notice.

CARRIE. I will.

ELSIE. No-one else will.

CARRIE. That's not the point.

ELSIE. It can be our secret.

CARRIE. Certainly not.

> ELSIE *tries to move.*

> Stand still.

ELSIE. It doesn't matter.

CARRIE. It does.

ELSIE. It's my wedding and I don't mind.

CARRIE. It must have come off the train.

> CARRIE *spreads out the train. It seems to fill the stage.*

ELSIE. What's the time?

CARRIE. Plenty of time.

ELSIE. Shouldn't you be outside overseeing?

CARRIE. You can't tempt me away.

ELSIE. If you haven't found it in one minute, I'm off.

CARRIE. Please stand still.

ELSIE. I can't. It's impossible. I'm too nervous.

CARRIE. You'll be alright.

ELSIE. One minute. I'm counting.

CARRIE. Got it! A gaping hole where a button should be.

ELSIE. Oh no.

CARRIE. Oh yes.

ELSIE. Leave it.

CARRIE. You must be perfect down to the last embroidered button.

ELSIE. I think it lends the dress an air of distinction.

CARRIE. Rubbish.

ELSIE. An intentional error – very modern.

>CARRIE *bends down with needle, thread, and button and addresses the problem.*

CARRIE. If you move about, I shall be slower.

ELSIE. Biarritz! Biarritz, Biarritz, Biarritz, Biarritz, Biarritz, Biarritz. It's one of those words you shouldn't say too often. You've been haven't you?

CARRIE. Yes, you'll have a lovely time.

ELSIE. We arrive in the middle of the night.

CARRIE. Stand still. Who will be there to meet you?

ELSIE. I've no idea.

CARRIE. Oh?

ELSIE. George has it all arranged. (*Pause.*) It's like 'what'.

CARRIE. What is?

ELSIE. 'What' – another word you shouldn't say too often. 'What, what, what, what, what, what.' Ceases to have any meaning.

>*There is a sound of breaking glass outside the window,* CARRIE *downs tools and races to the window.*

CARRIE. Oh Lord.

>ELSIE *tries to make an escape.*

Don't you dare. Come back.

>ELSIE *is nearly out, but her exit is blocked by* RUDYARD*'s appearance at the door. He has aged dramatically. He seems smaller and frailer. This is his first glimpse of the wedding dress.*

(*To* RUDYARD.) Well?

RUDYARD. Oh . . . very . . . fine . . .

ELSIE. 'Fine'?

RUDYARD. Well . . .

ELSIE. Funny word. Do you like it?

RUDYARD. Oh yes . . . yes.

    RUDYARD *looks flustered*.

ELSIE. It's silk . . . twenty yards of silk.

RUDYARD. Yes, splendid. Practically the length of a cricket pitch.

    CARRIE *has finished the button*.

CARRIE. There we are. All done.

ELSIE. Thank you.

CARRIE (*kissing* ELSIE). You look beautiful.

RUDYARD. You do indeed.

CARRIE (*looking out of the window*). Oh Lord. Glass everywhere. (*To* RUDYARD.) You sit down and admire your daughter for a moment. (CARRIE *leads* RUDYARD *to a chair*.) How are the inside cupboards?

RUDYARD (*feeling his stomach*). A little disarranged, but I'm fine.

CARRIE. There's a brand new packet of Jenner's Absorbent Lozenges in your pocket.

RUDYARD. Thank you.

CARRIE. Take one now please.

RUDYARD. I will, fear not.

CARRIE. Now please.

    RUDYARD *extricates the packet and takes one*.

RUDYARD (*to* ELSIE). I hope George doesn't exercise such tyranny.

CARRIE (*to* RUDYARD). For your own good. I'll fetch you when we're ready to leave.

    CARRIE *goes. A short silence*.

RUDYARD. Mother's eyes are dancing again, thanks to you.

ELSIE. Are they? Perhaps I should go and help her.

RUDYARD. No need I'm sure.

ELSIE. I can't sit down. I can't move around. I can't stand still.

RUDYARD. Not long now . . . I'm wondering if the aisle will be wide enough for the three of us.

ELSIE. Three?

RUDYARD. You and I, and twenty yards of silk.

ELSIE. Oh.

RUDYARD. Perhaps I shall disappear from view altogether. Only the top of my head visible, bobbing along within a sea of white silk.

ELSIE laughs.

ELSIE. But it looks alright?

RUDYARD. Yes . . .

ELSIE. You don't sound . . .

RUDYARD. Oh yes, it's splendid.

Silence.

So you 'P. & O.' it to Calais?

ELSIE. Yes.

RUDYARD. Then a train direct to Biarritz?

ELSIE. Yes.

RUDYARD. I envy you. There is something stately and massive about a French train. It is one of the delights of the age . . . but for one small detail.

ELSIE. What's that?

RUDYARD. No porridge and kippers for breakfast. Just cold, flaky pastry.

ELSIE. I like their pastry.

RUDYARD. When will the house in Brussels be ready?

ELSIE. It won't. It's completely empty. We have to start from scratch.

RUDYARD. I want to be consulted on every decision. Curtains, colours . . . artworks . . . bookshelves . . .

ELSIE. You'll be our House of Lords, you'll have the final veto.

RUDYARD. I want to know everything relating to you and your doings – long letters please – or we shall abandon you to the Belgians, which would not be kind.

ELSIE. Do you think you'll move?

RUDYARD. Good Lord no . . . room to breathe at last.

Short silence.

And if there's any furniture . . . or . . . whatever . . . here . . . that would be useful, just say the word – we'll ship it over.

ELSIE. Thank you, I'm sure we'll be fine.

RUDYARD. Well, you may think of something . . . what about the billiard table, that would cause a stir on the continent.

ELSIE. I'm sure we'll be fine . . . what do you think the time is?

RUDYARD. Mother will collect us, fear not.

Silence.

ELSIE. I wish I could sit down.

RUDYARD. Why don't you?

ELSIE. I'm going to.

She perches uncomfortably somewhere. Long silence. Just the sound of preparations outside.

RUDYARD. Do you know what a 'Doli' is?

ELSIE. No.

RUDYARD. It's a Hindu wedding ceremony.

ELSIE. A 'Doli'?

RUDYARD. I saw one once in Lahore . . . my Father was curator of the city museum.

ELSIE. Yes.

RUDYARD. And I would sneak off when he wasn't looking, and prowl down the lanes near the Delhi Gate. On one occasion, I came upon a bridegroom and his family wheeling a cart full of huge, bright cushions, down the street. They were on their way to collect the bride and bear her away on the cart. This is the 'Doli.'

ELSIE. Right.

RUDYARD. So I stuck with them. I followed them. And eventually we turned into a narrow dark street . . . and there they were, waiting, the bride and her parents, standing on the front doorstep of a tiny flat-roofed house – waiting for the groom. The bride was in the middle, dressed in her Shalwar-Kameez, paid for and provided by the groom's family. The mother stood on the bride's left, dry-eyed and very still, but the bride's father was wailing and howling, the tears were pouring down his face, grief, terrible grief, he was losing his beloved daughter. His arms were around her waist, he clung to her, he buried his head in her bosom, and his tears left wet patches on the front of her silk shirt. He was inconsolable. And this is expected, this the father is allowed to do at the Hindu 'Doli'.

Silence.

ELSIE. I'm sorry.

RUDYARD. What for?

ELSIE. Well . . .

RUDYARD. We'll be fine.

ELSIE. It's not as if we're moving to India or Africa . . .

RUDYARD. Bird we'll be fine. But they're interesting . . . none the less . . . these cultural differences . . . there is a Punjabi saying: 'Daughters are only visitors.'

ELSIE. How depressing.

RUDYARD. Do you think so?

ELSIE. What does it mean anyway?

RUDYARD. Property of the groom I suppose.

ELSIE. How awful. Thank God I'm English.

RUDYARD. Well, yes! Indeed. Thank God.

They laugh, then relapse into silence.

Allah be praised. Thank God we're English.

They laugh again – blackout.

End of Scene Four.

ACT TWO SCENE FIVE

1933.

RUDYARD *and* CARRIE *are elderly and frail. They sit alone, listening to the wireless.*

BBC NEWSREADER. Good evening. This is the BBC. Here is the news, copyright reserved, on Monday January 30th 1933. This morning at 11.00 a.m. Adolf Hitler was appointed Chancellor of Germany. His party, the National Socialist German Workers' Party, has captured one third of the national vote in the General Elections and will become the largest group in the new Reichstag. Of Hitler's triumph, Joseph Goebbels said today:

'It's like a dream, the great decision has been taken. The nation erupts! Germany is awake! The German revolution begins!'

RUDYARD *switches off the wireless – he sits back in his chair.*

RUDYARD. For nothing, for nothing, for nothing.

Silence. Then, as if children were in the room.

Kiddos. Kiddos. I am glad to the limits of gladness to see you. I rejoice to the uttermost extent of rejoicing. Did you have a 'Snipspus' tea? Do you know what I had? . . . Gruel with no rice. And fouler still – Tapioca for pud . . . Do you want a story?

Silence.

'Have you news of my boy Jack?'
Not this tide.
'When d'you think that he'll come back?'
Not with this wind blowing, and this tide.

'Has any one else had word of him?'
Not this tide.
For what is sunk will hardly swim,
Not with this wind blowing, and this tide.

'Oh dear, what comfort can I find?'
None this tide
Nor any tide
Except he did not shame his kind –
Not even with that wind blowing and that tide.

Then hold your head up all the more
This tide,
And every tide,
Because he was the son you bore
And gave to that wind blowing and that tide.

The End.